doodle all the day-o

a coloring book for the young and old alike

by Kelly Maddern

mad
INGENUITY

Published by madingenuity
©2015 - Waukesha, WI
www.madingenuity.com

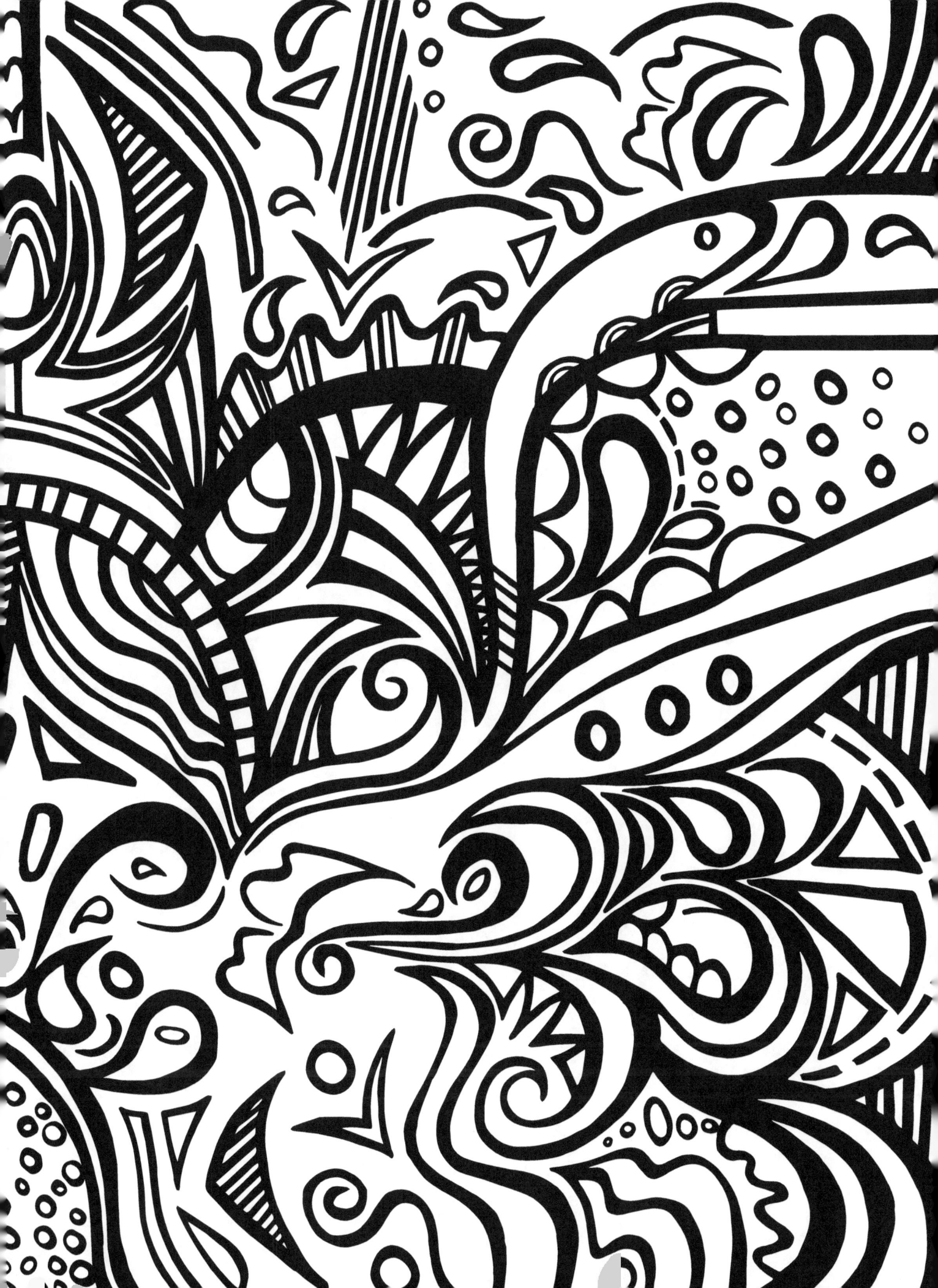

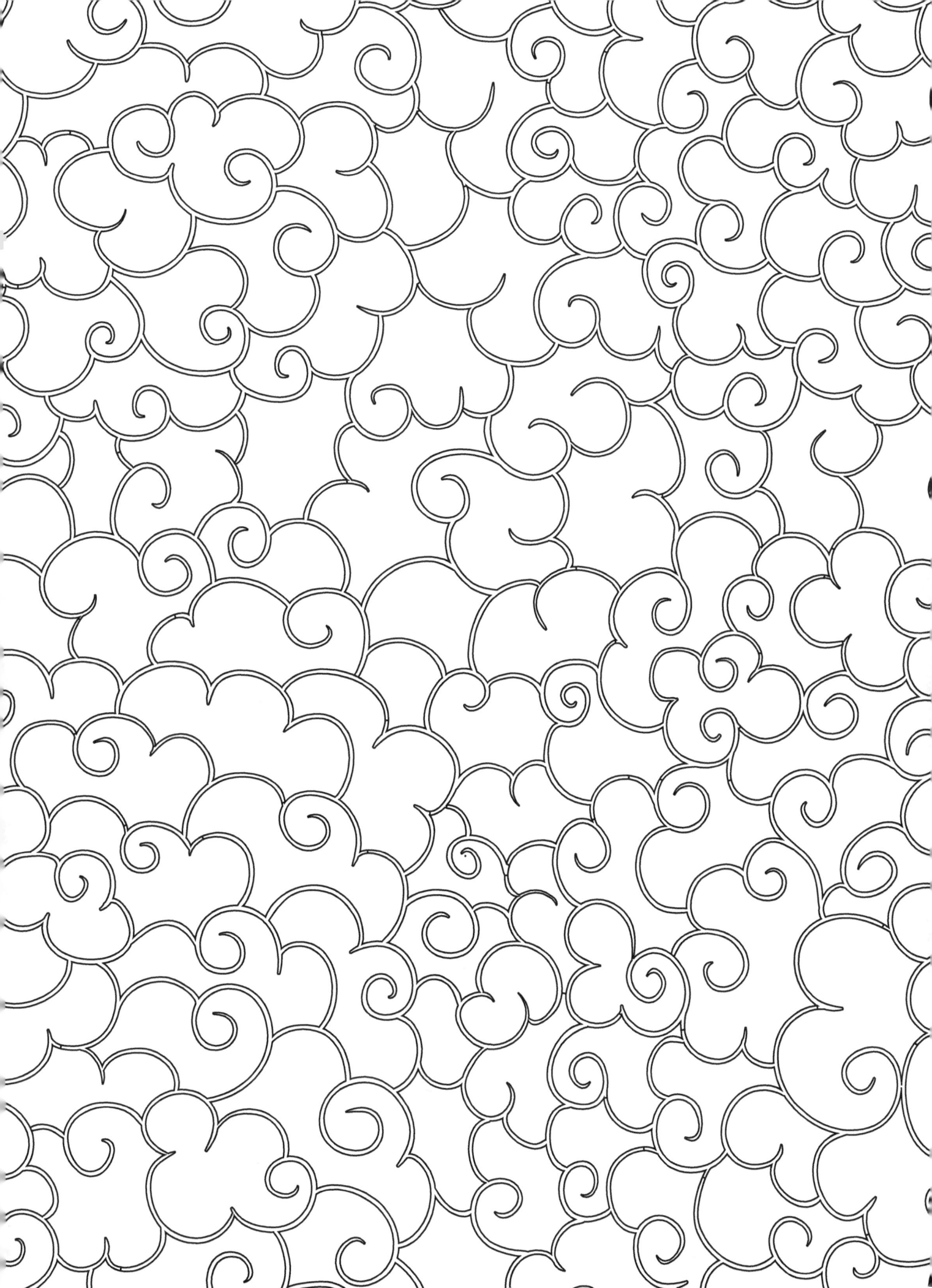

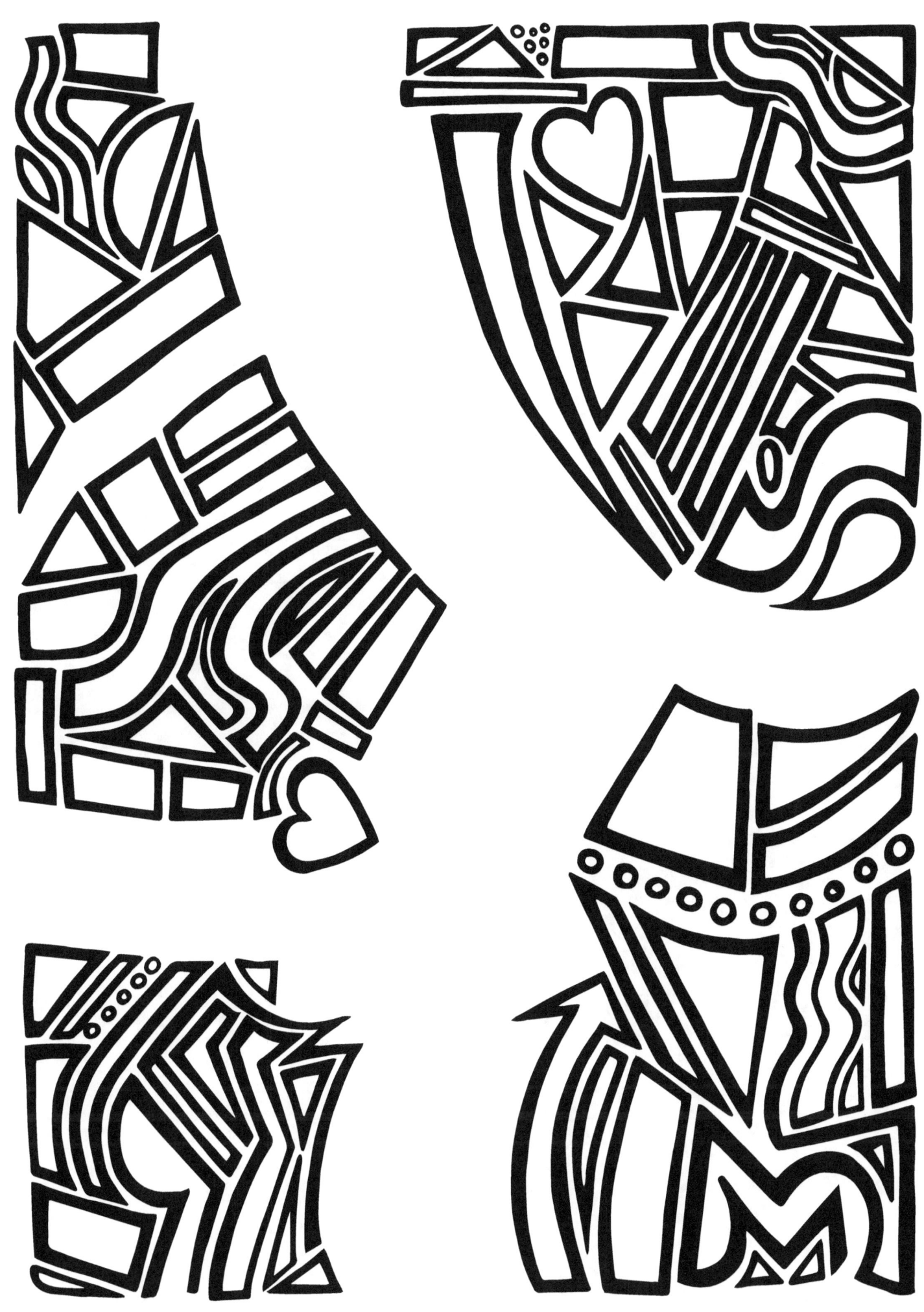

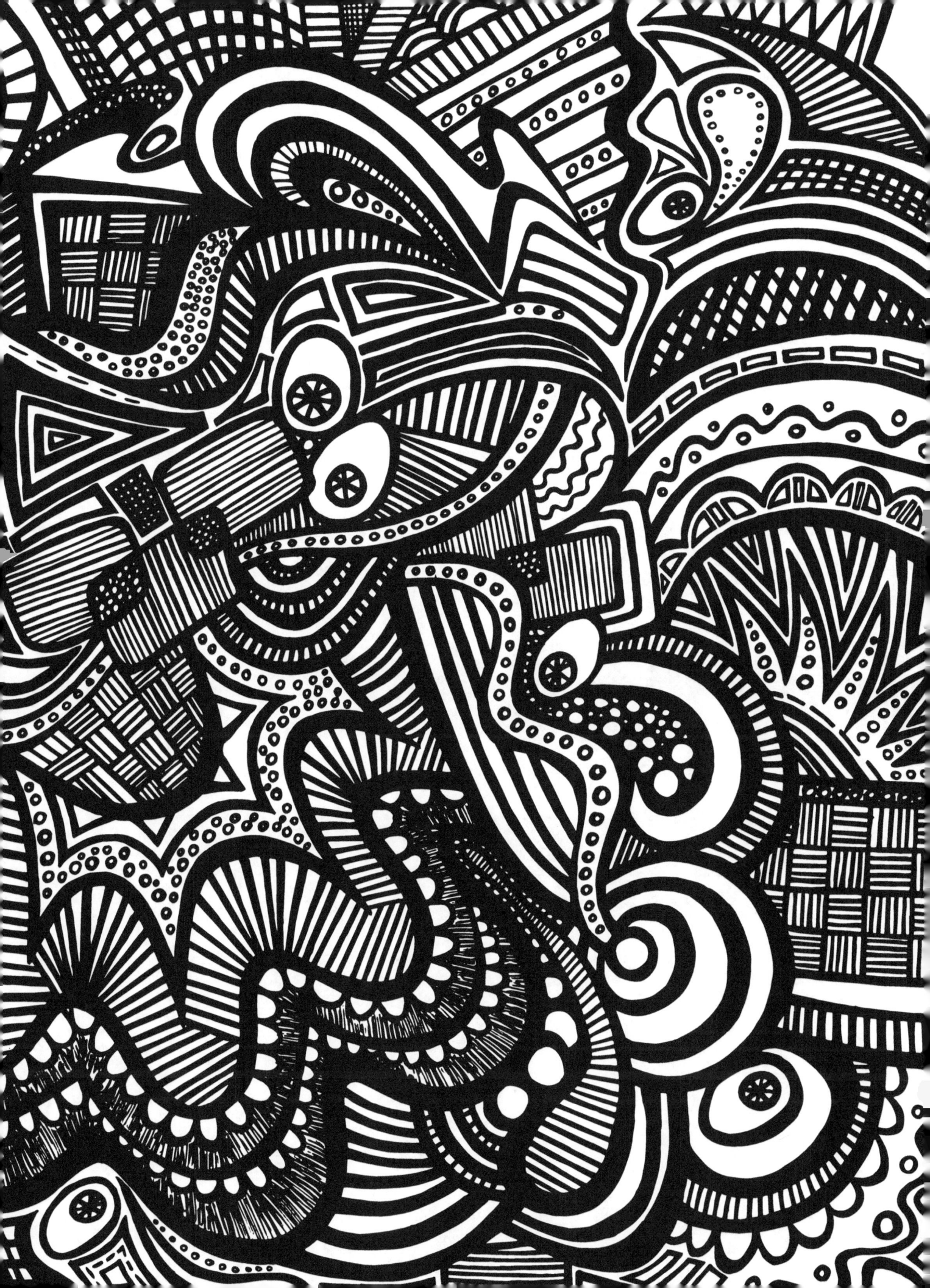

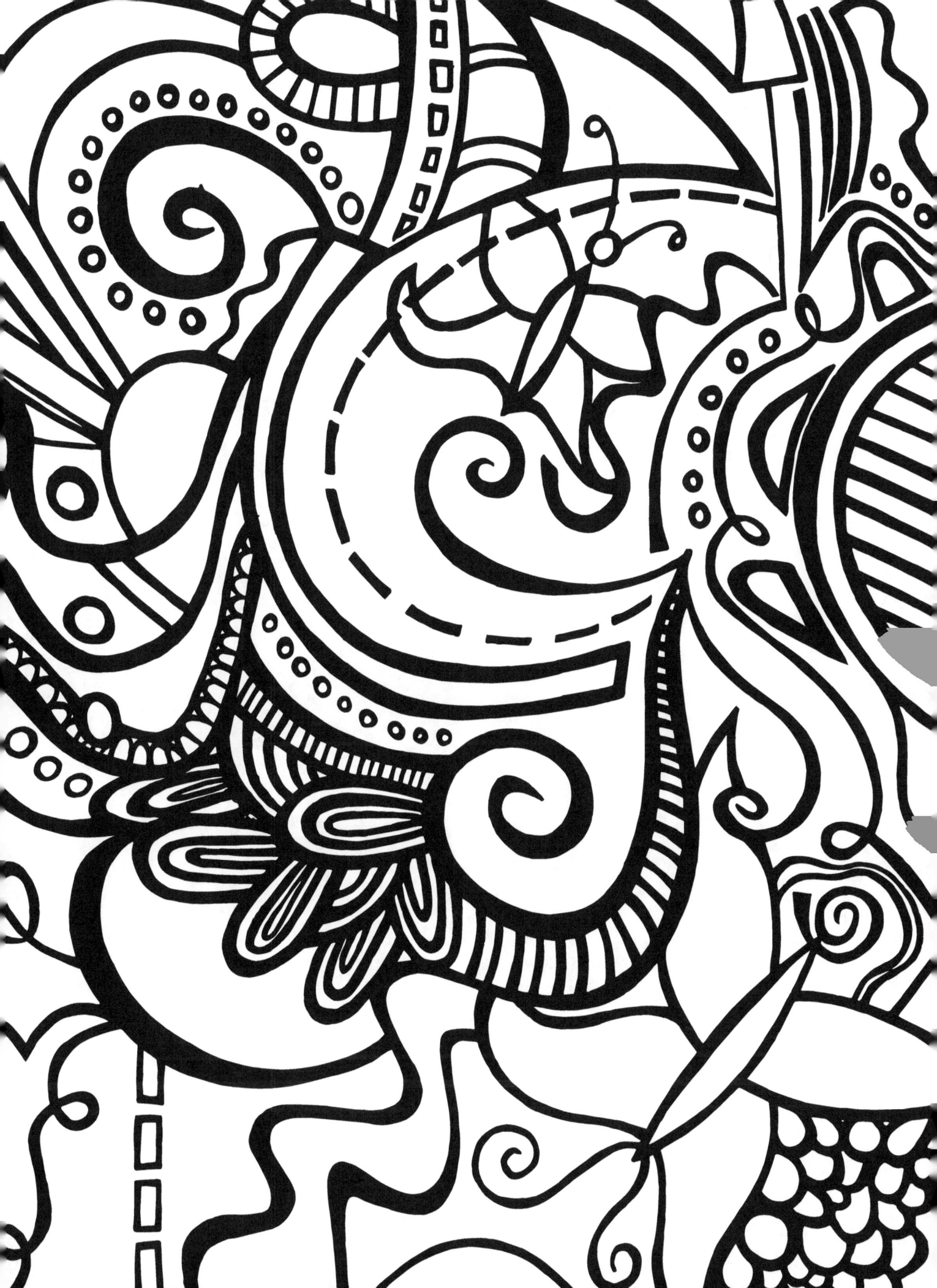

heRe aRe the nOn-RuLes Of thiS BoOk:

• You DO NOT have to work in order... start wherever you want–wherever your mood takes you.

• White Space - color it, fill it with text, make your own doodles or leave it as-is! (I purposely left some blanks for your creativity!)

• You will notice a few pages that are repeated. This is NOT a mistake. It will give you an opportunity to color the first one and then color the other in a completely different way. Think of it as a way to go outside of your comfort zone!

• Before you start coloring, take a moment to think about the image. The image could be a variety of different things depending on how you choose to color it.

• Stumped or frustrated with how to color a page? Move on!

ReLax • Be cReative • ShaRe!

Your finished pages will inspire others and show how many different ways one page can look.

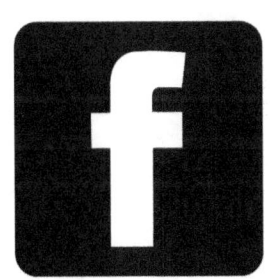

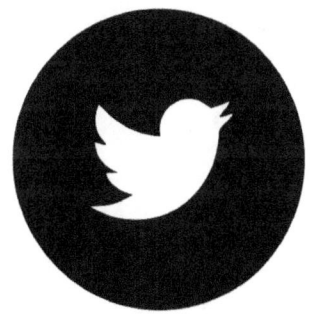

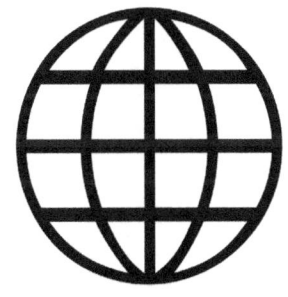

facebook.com/
DoodleAllTheDayO

@doodlealldayo
#mydayopage

doodlealltheday-o.com

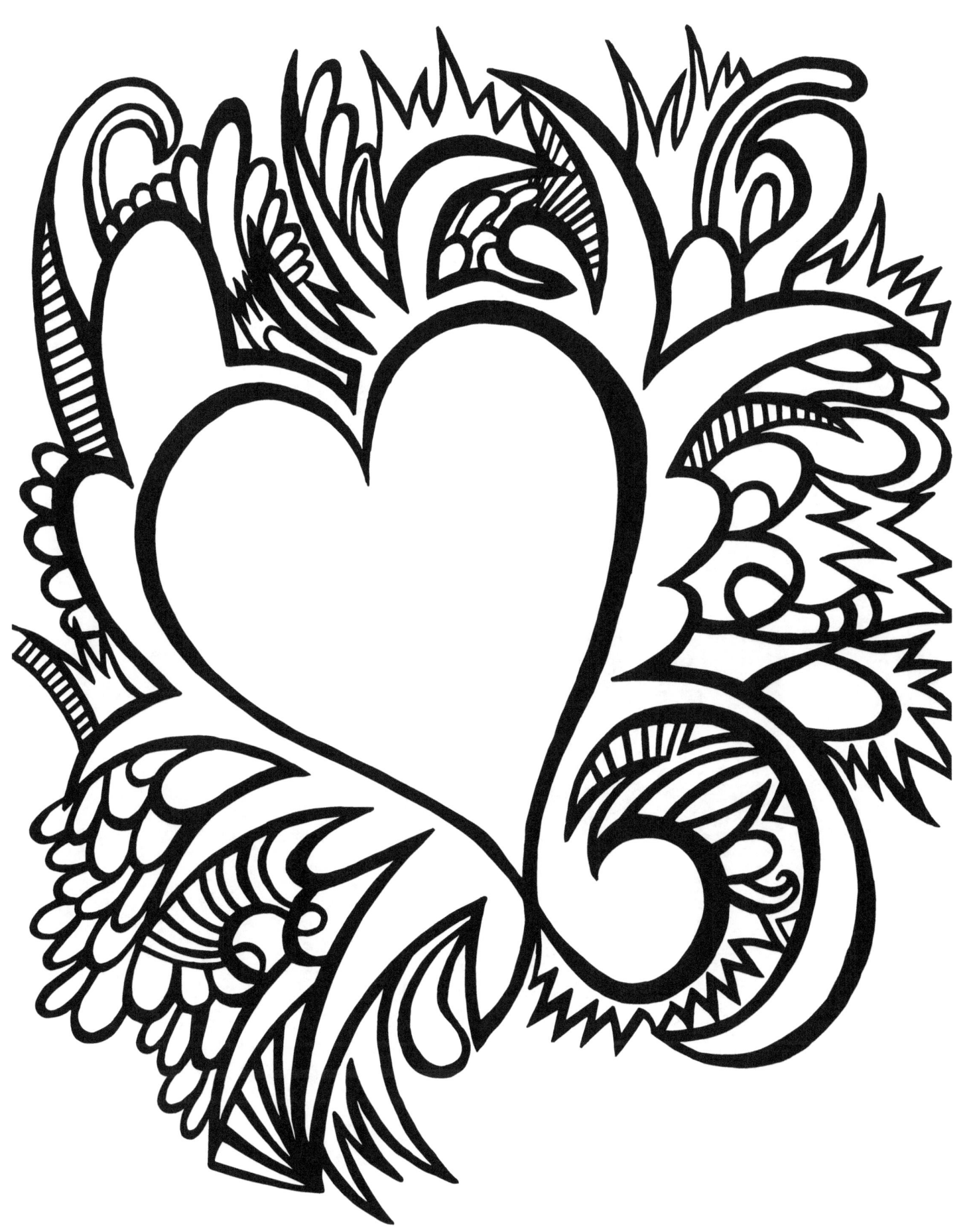

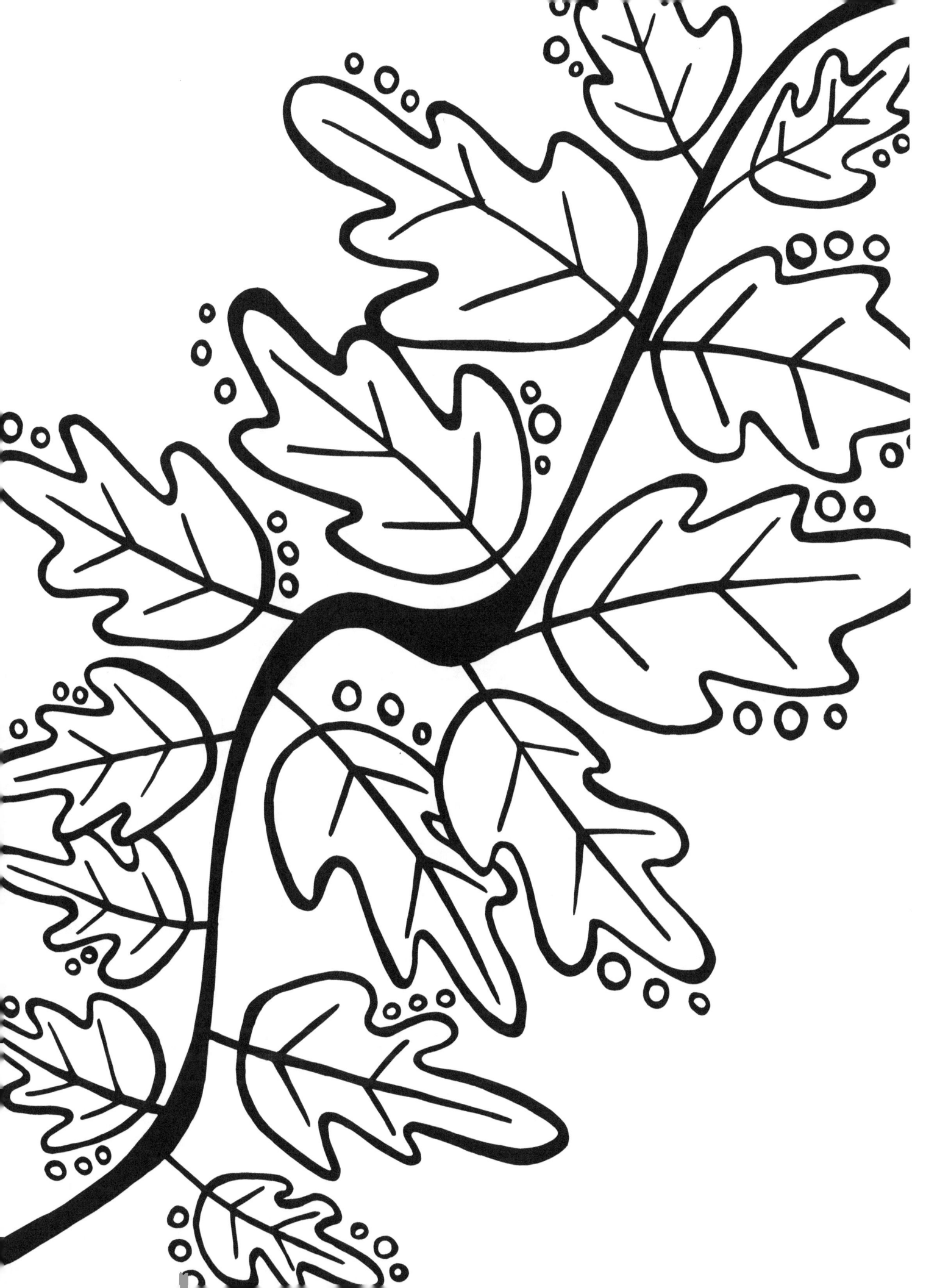

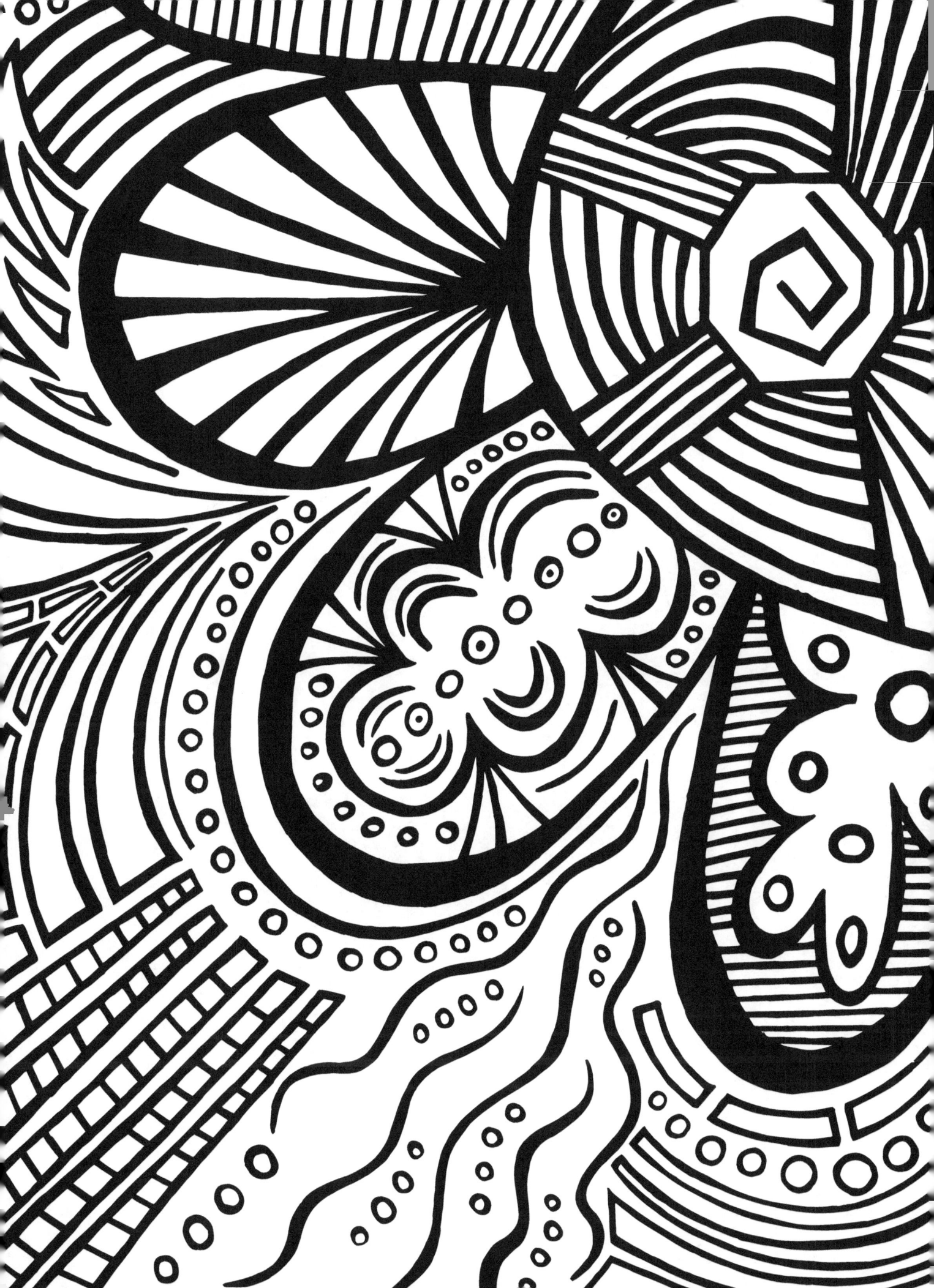

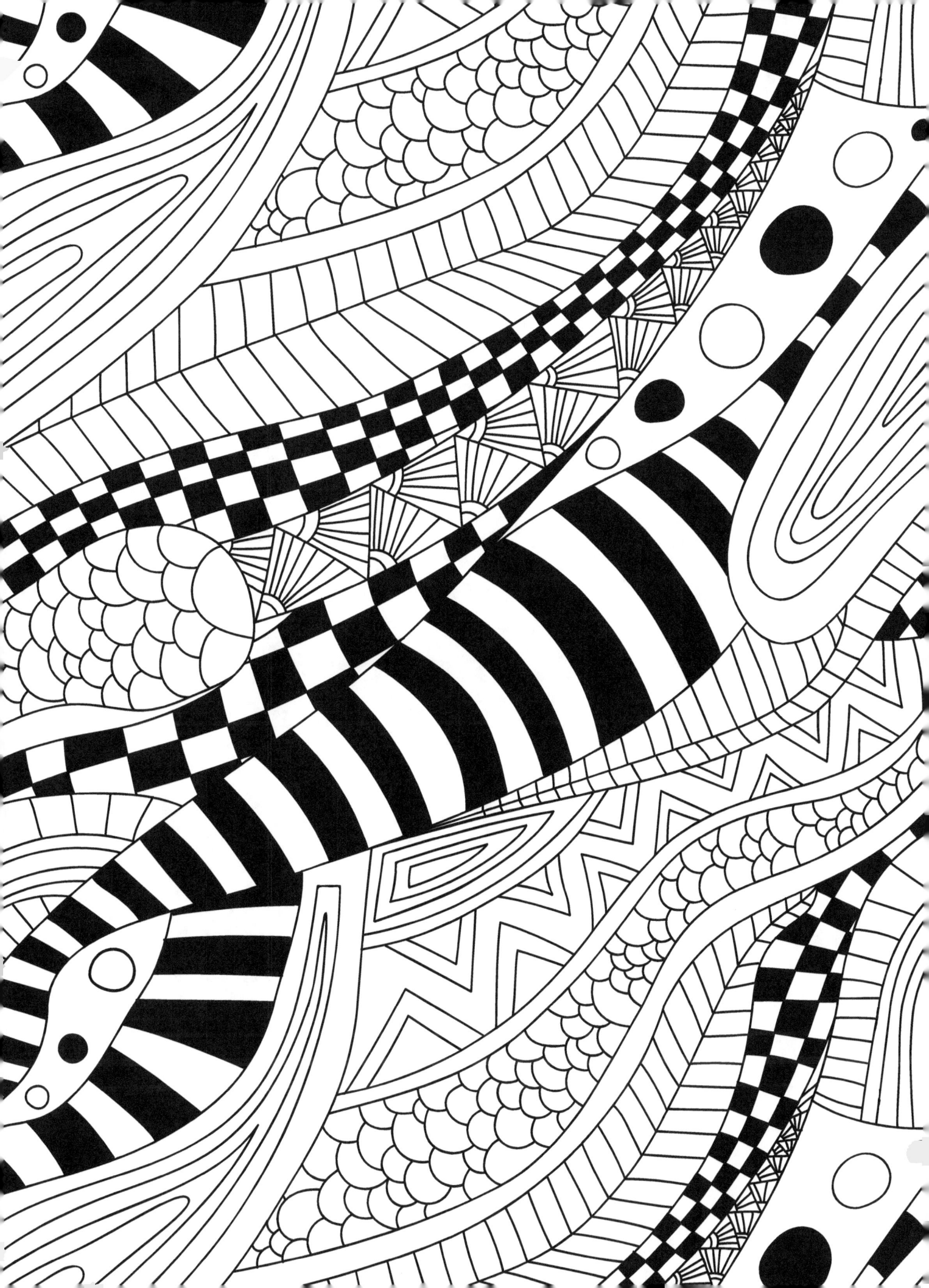

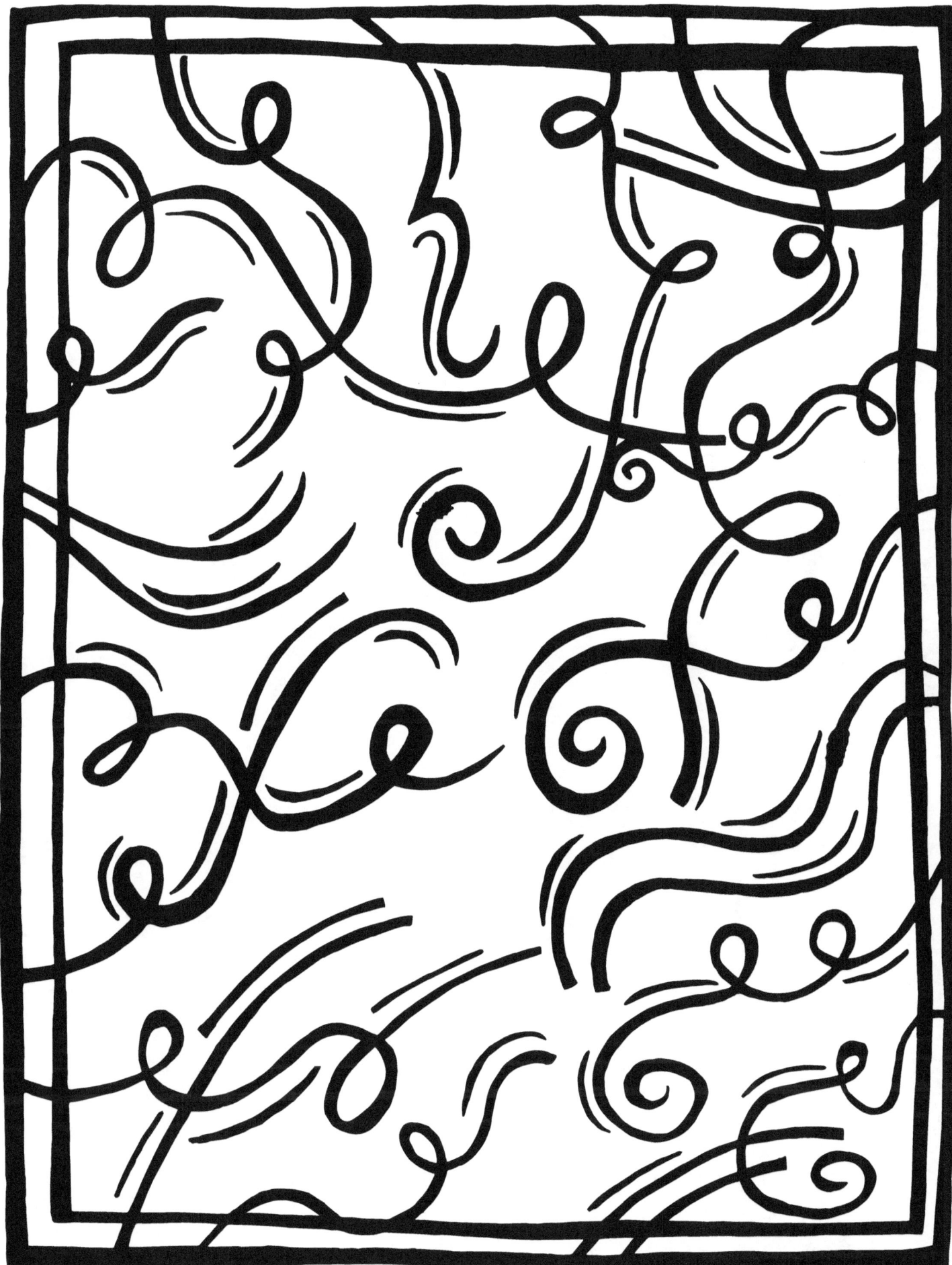

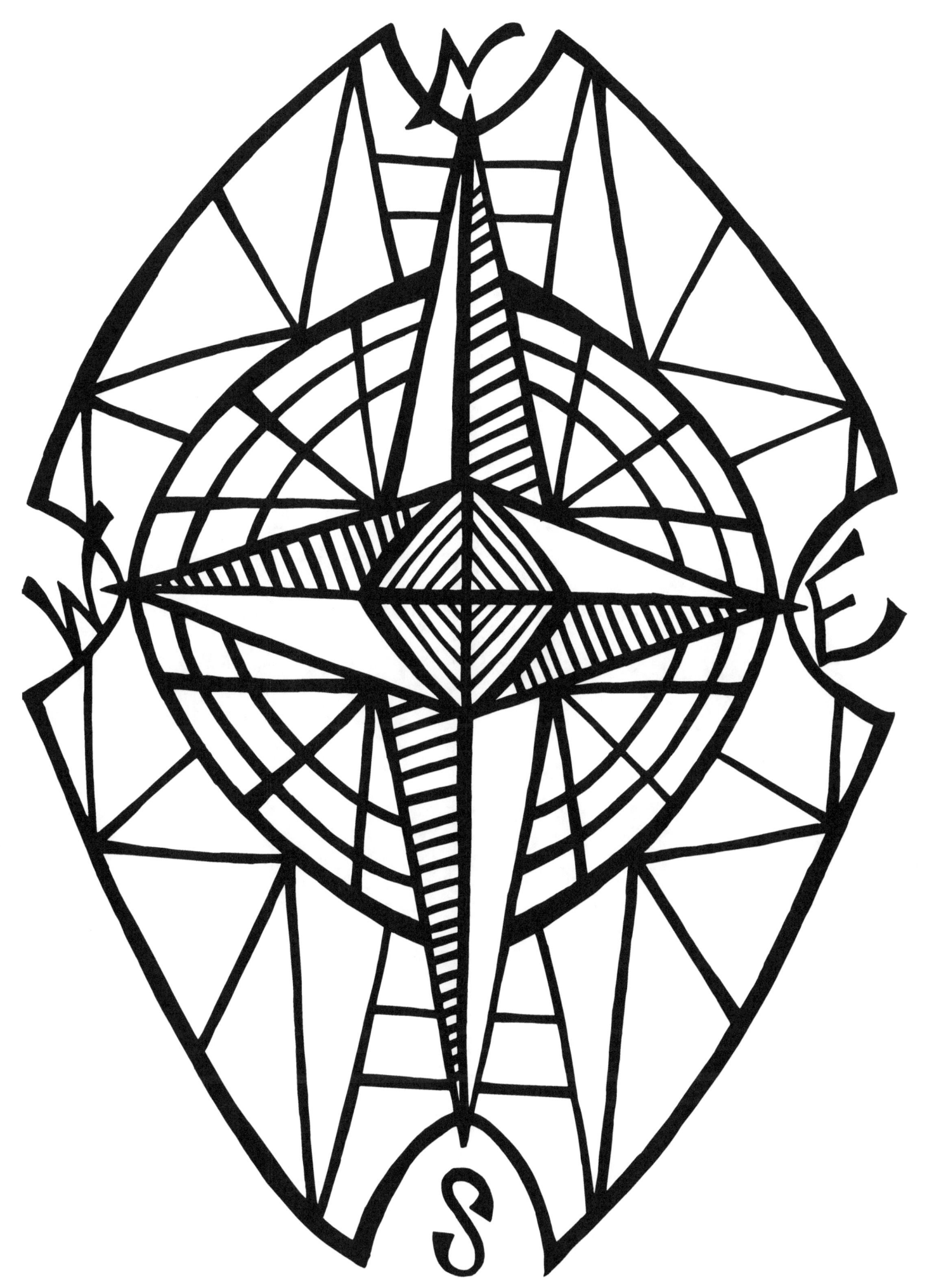

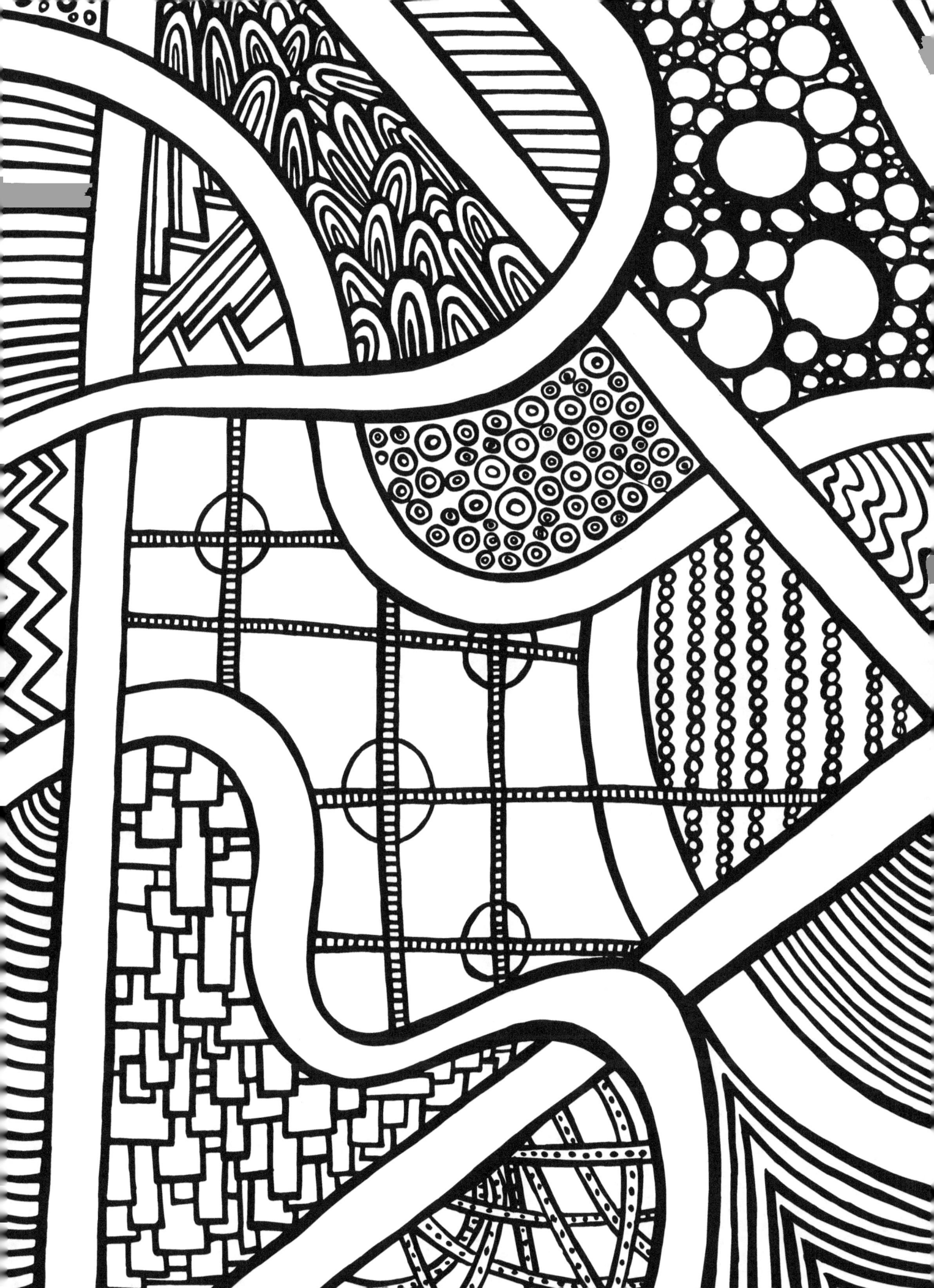

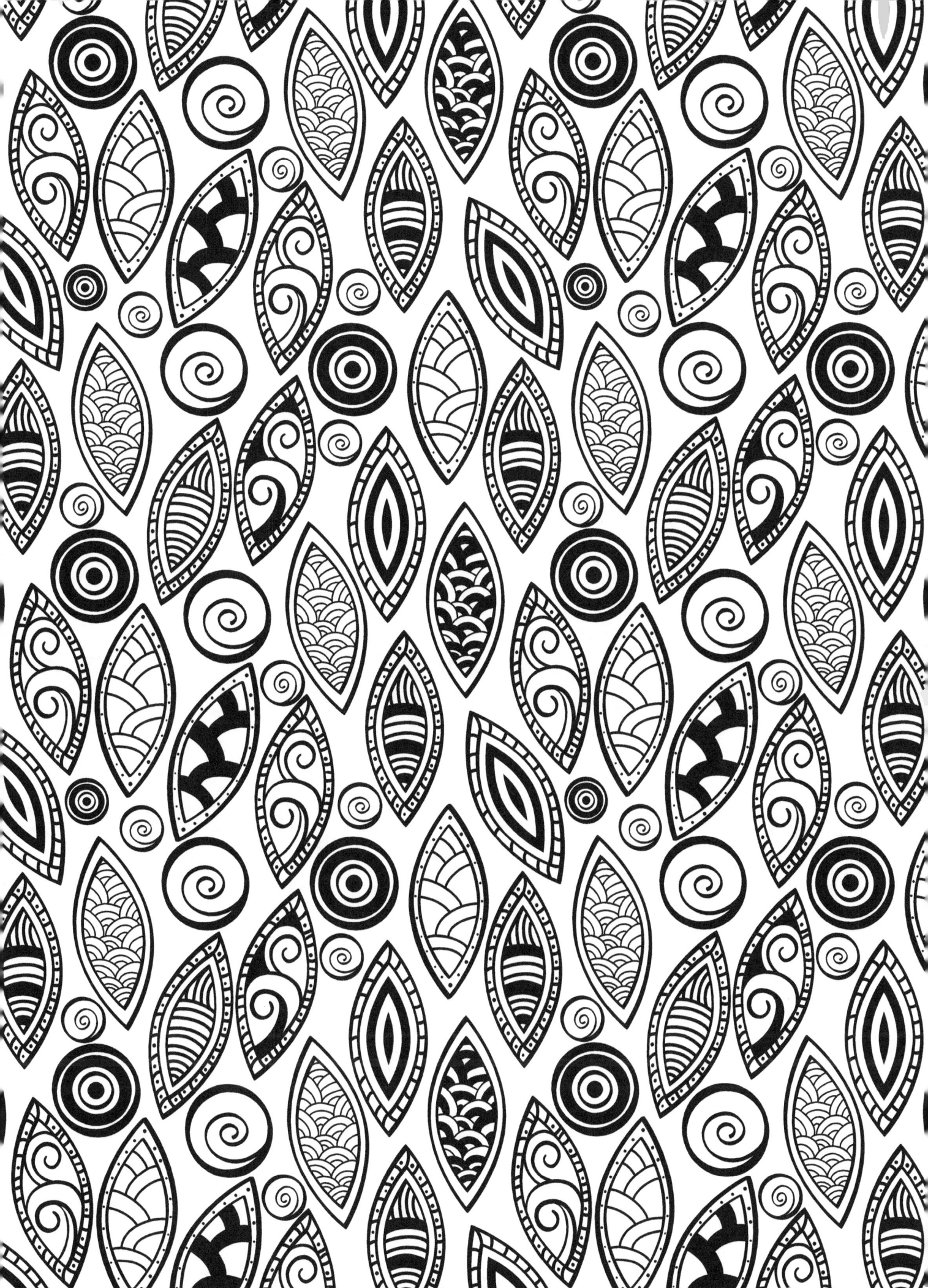

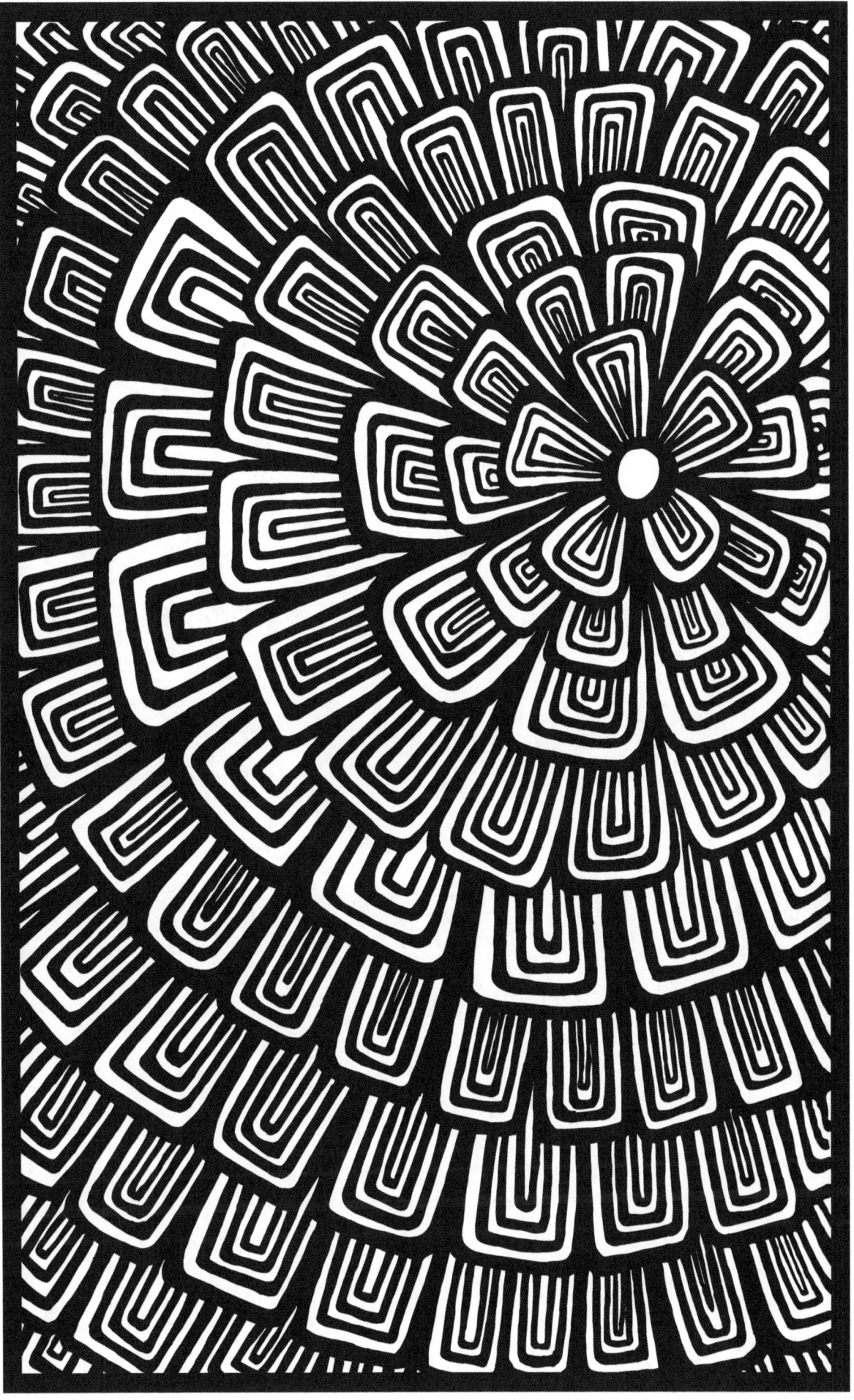

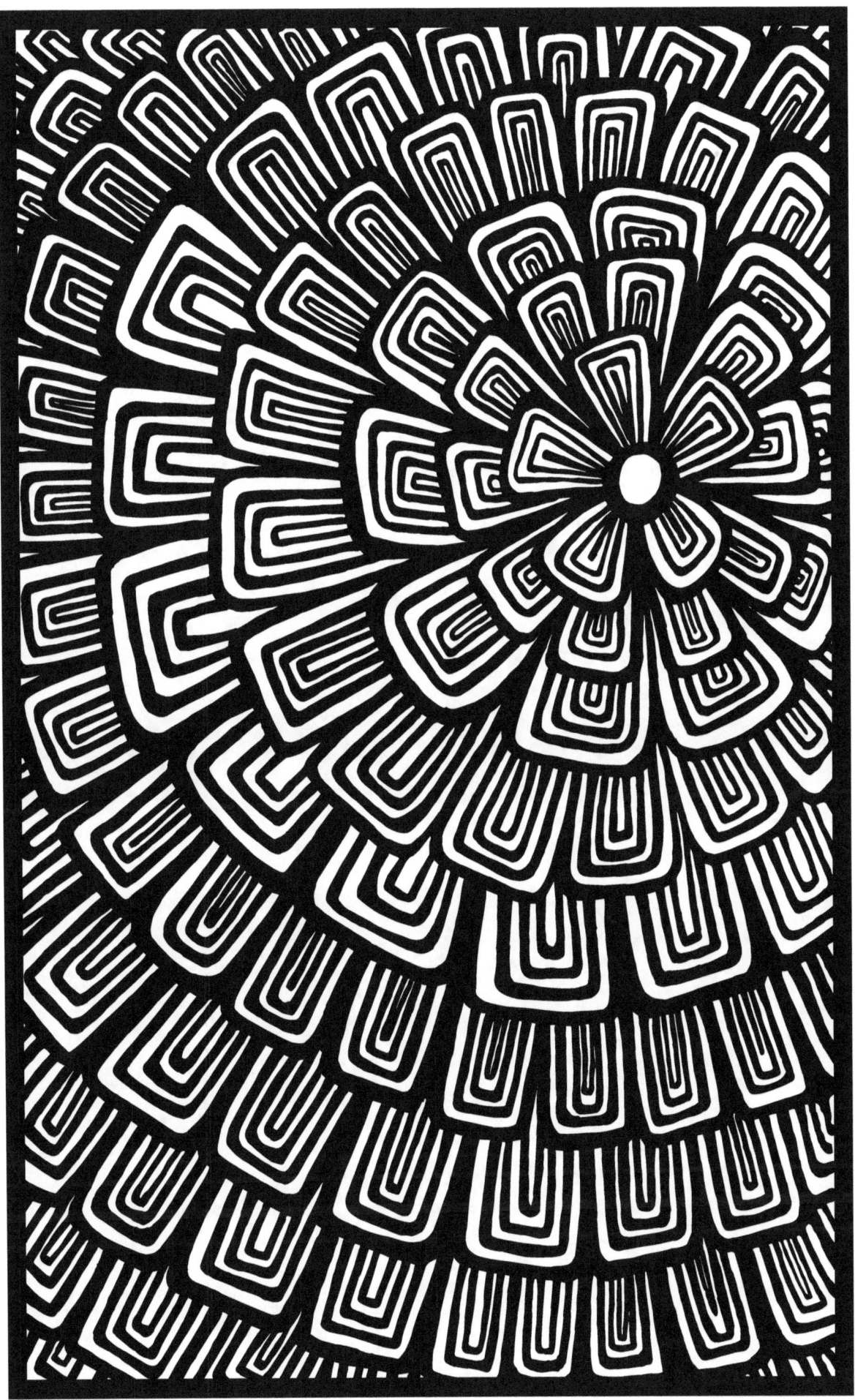

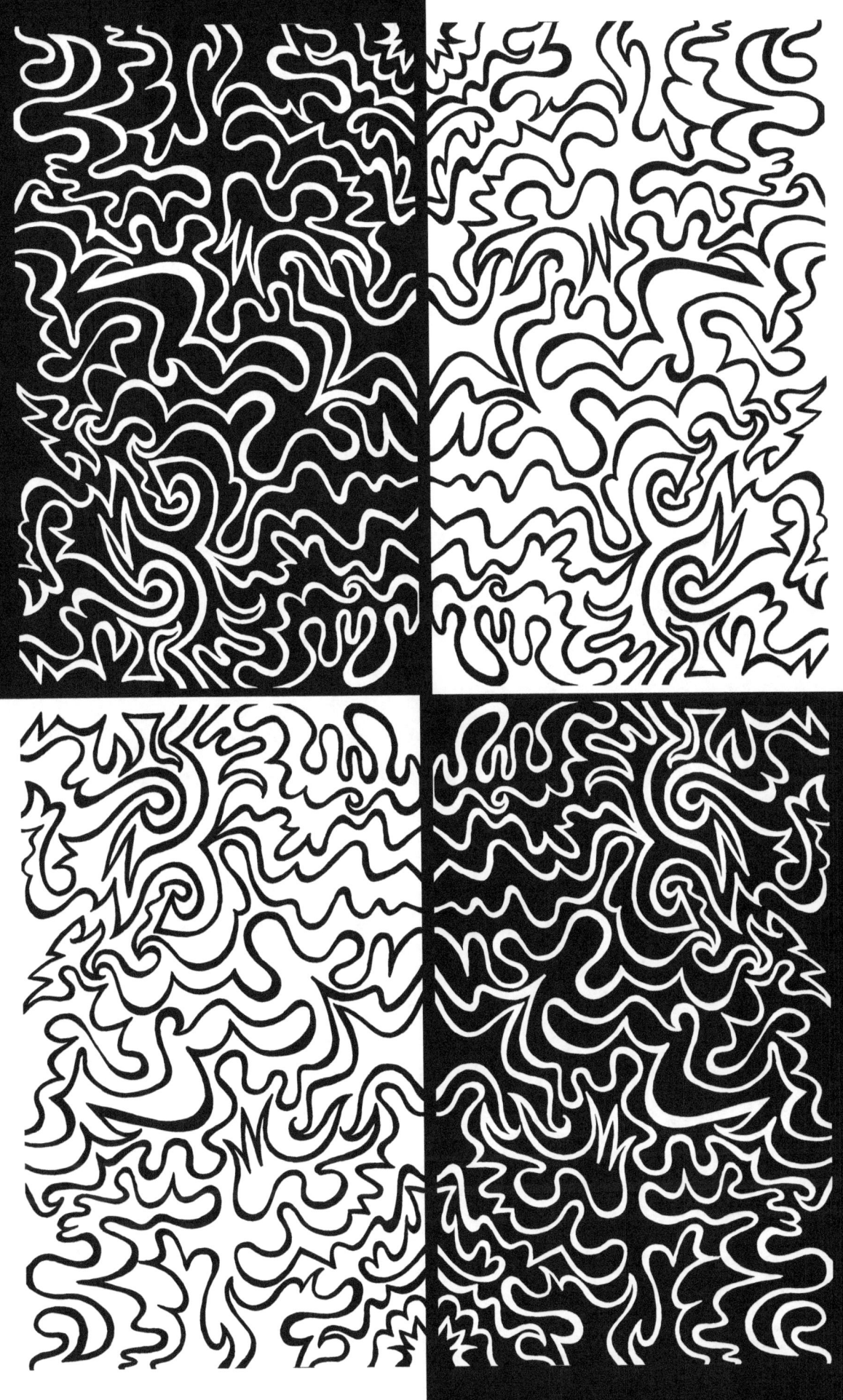

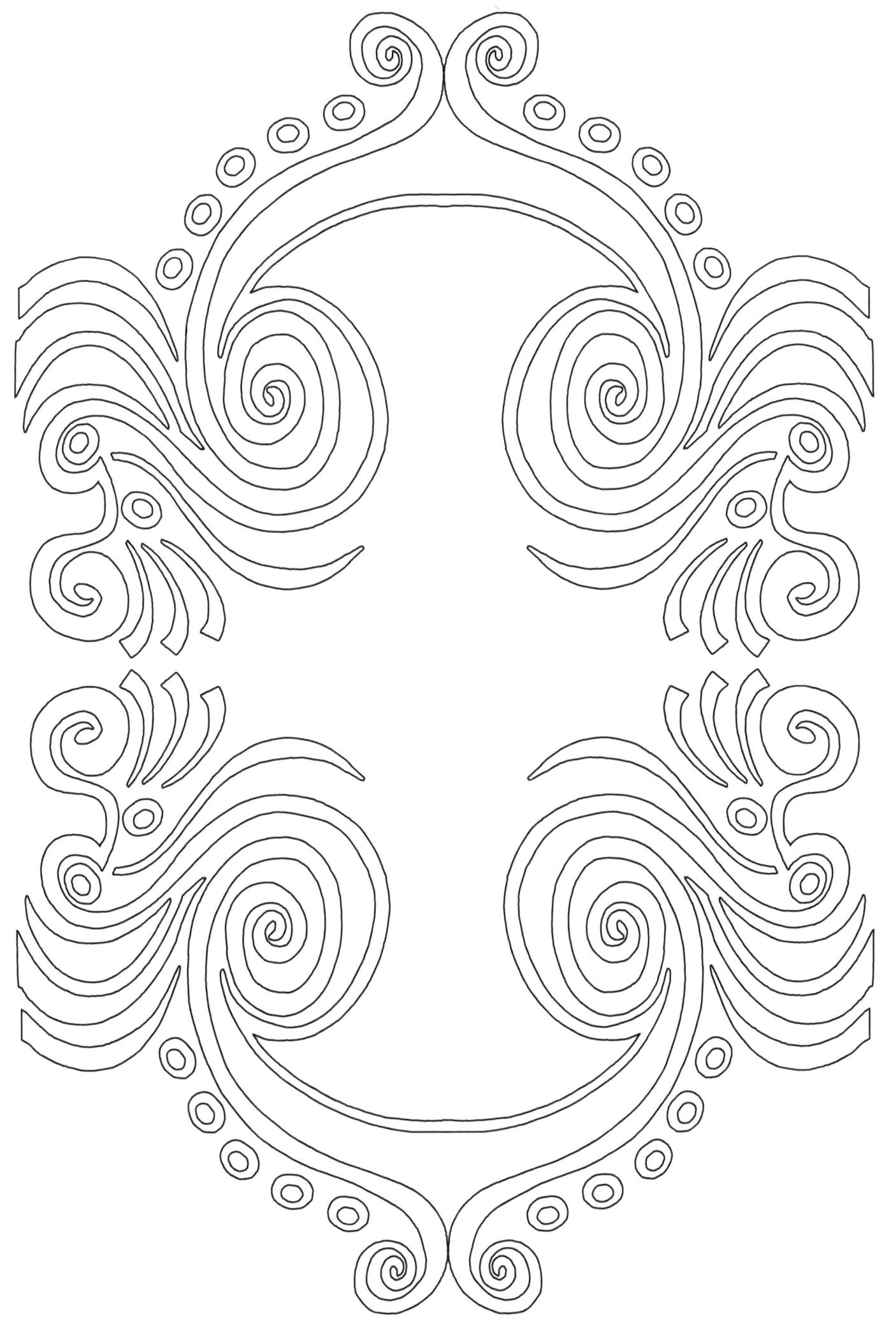

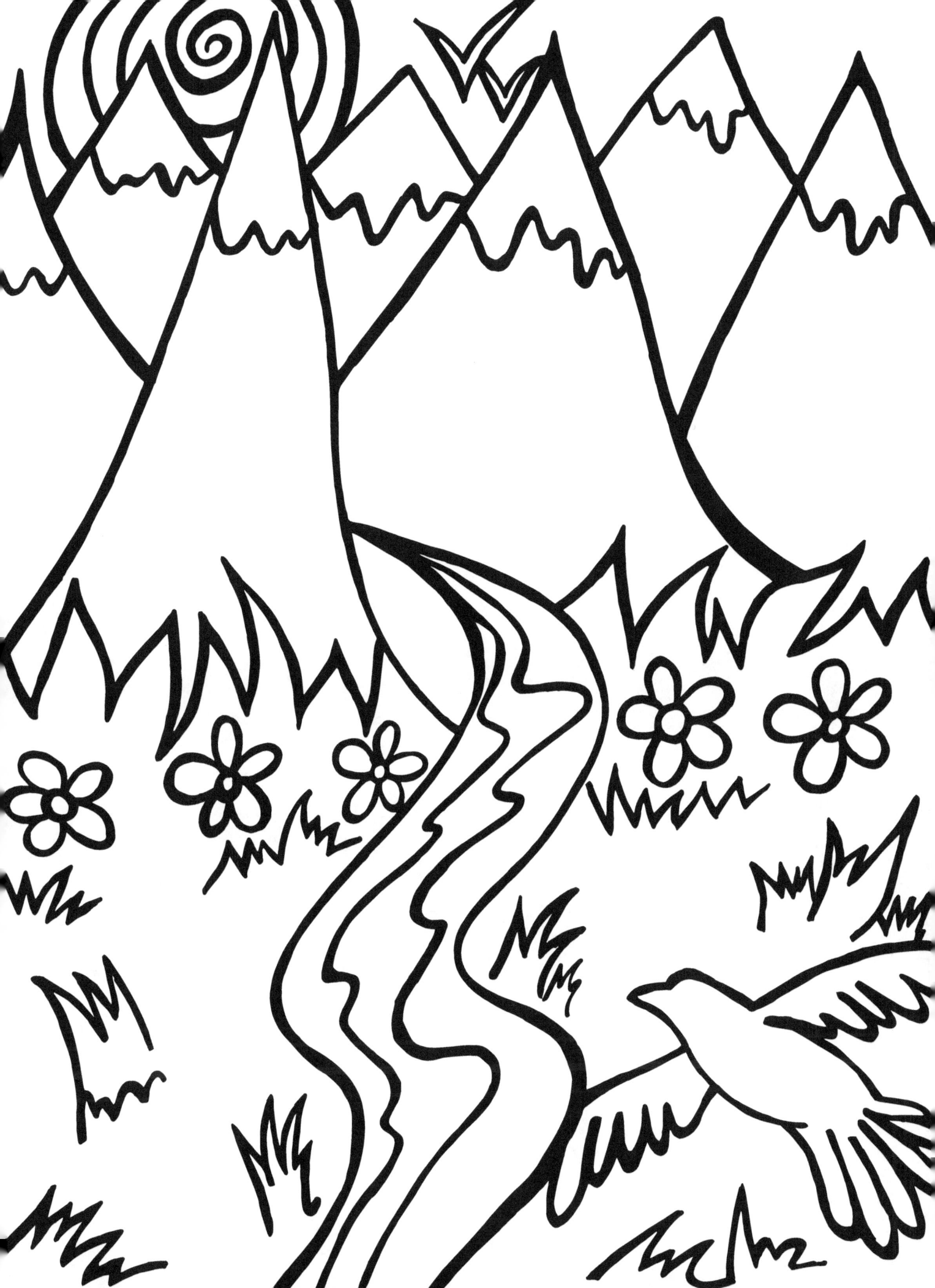

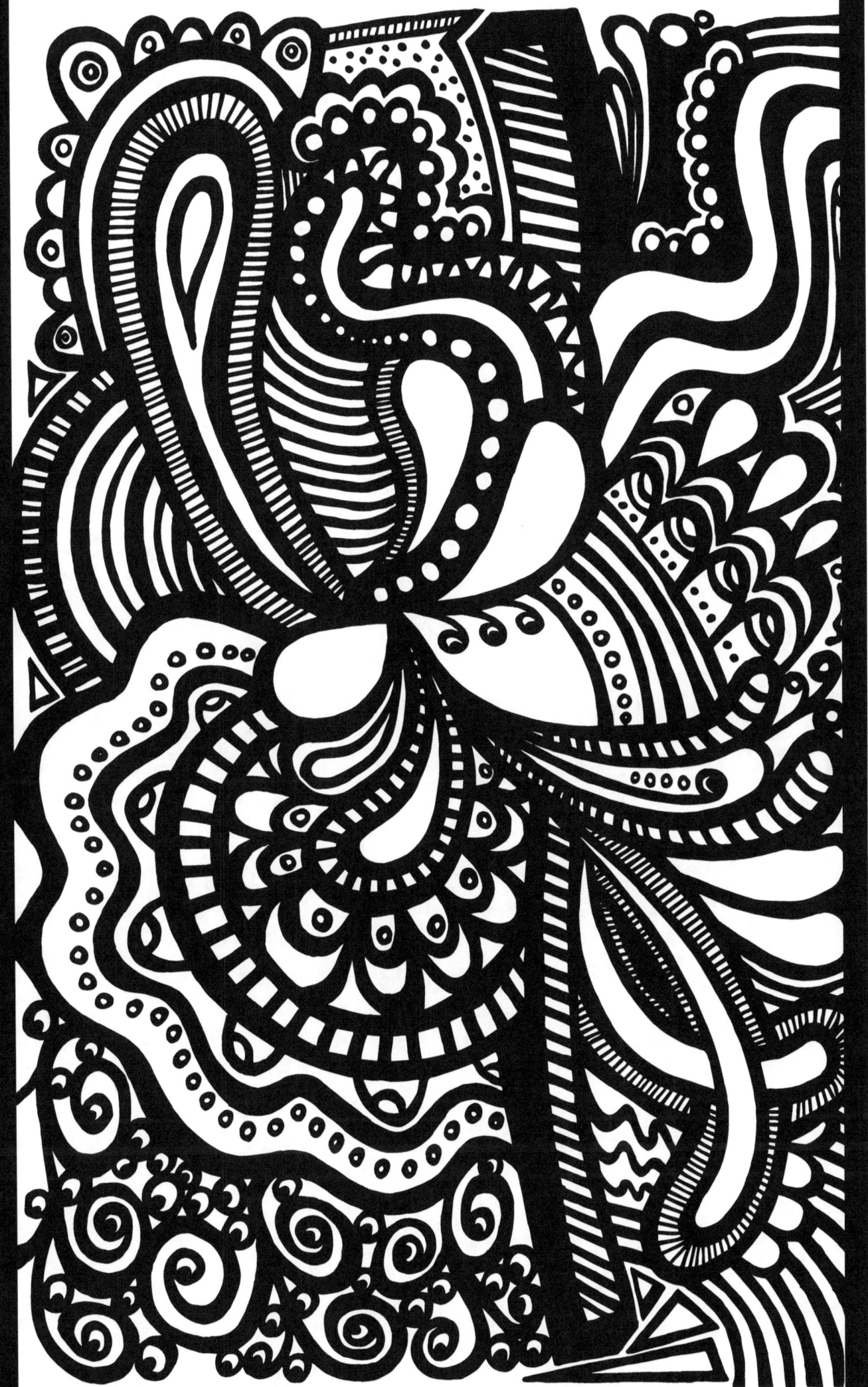

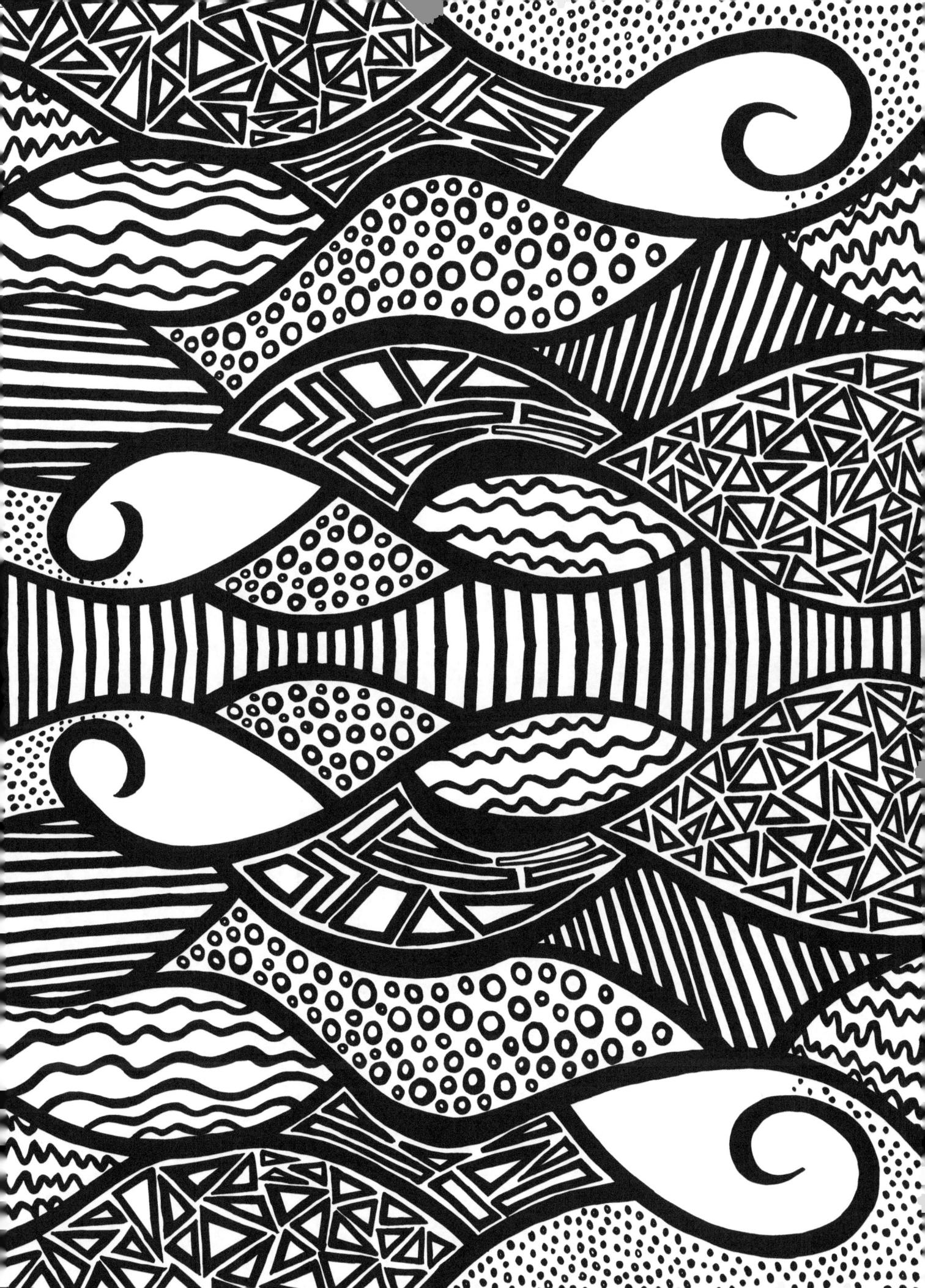

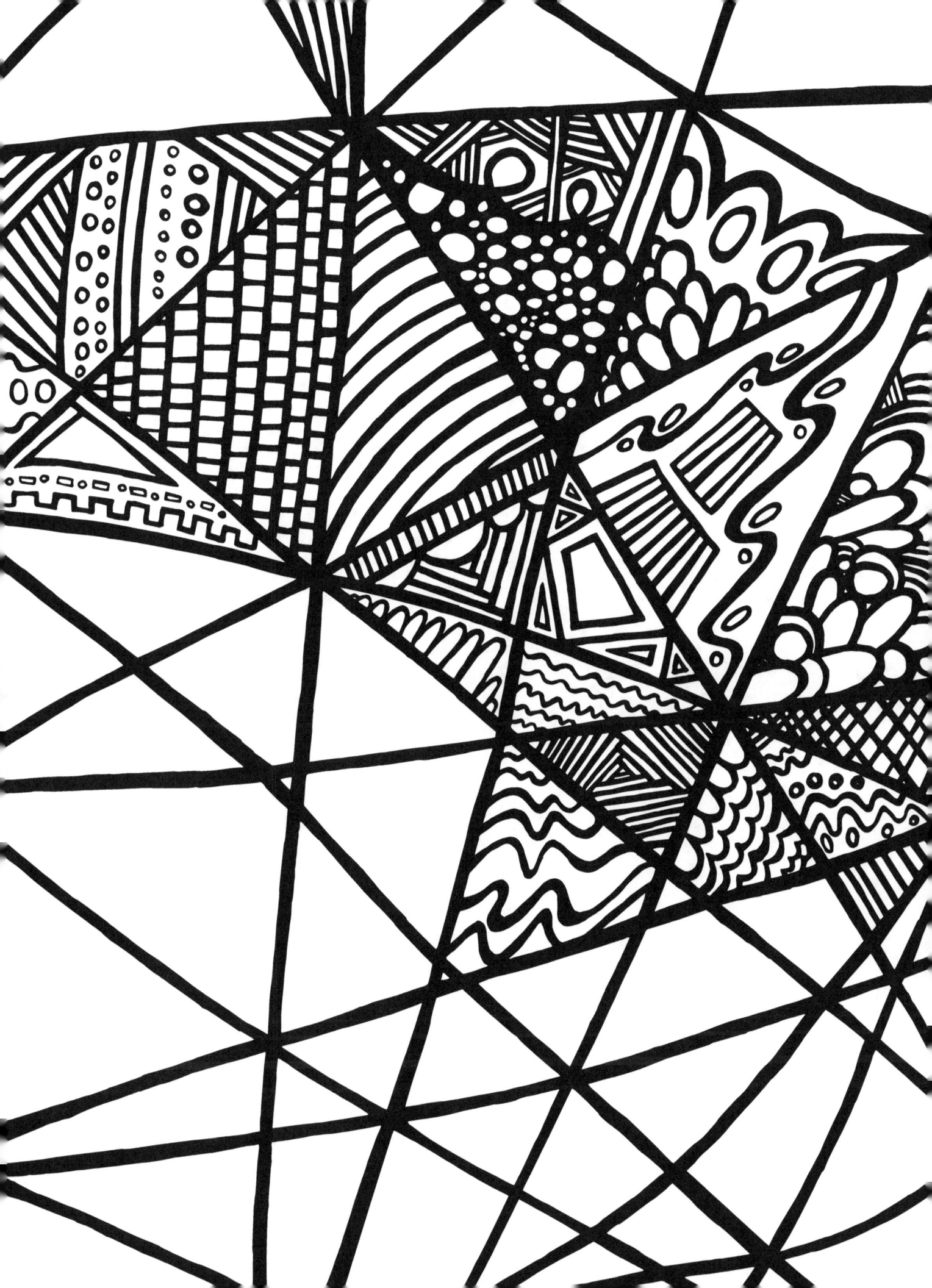

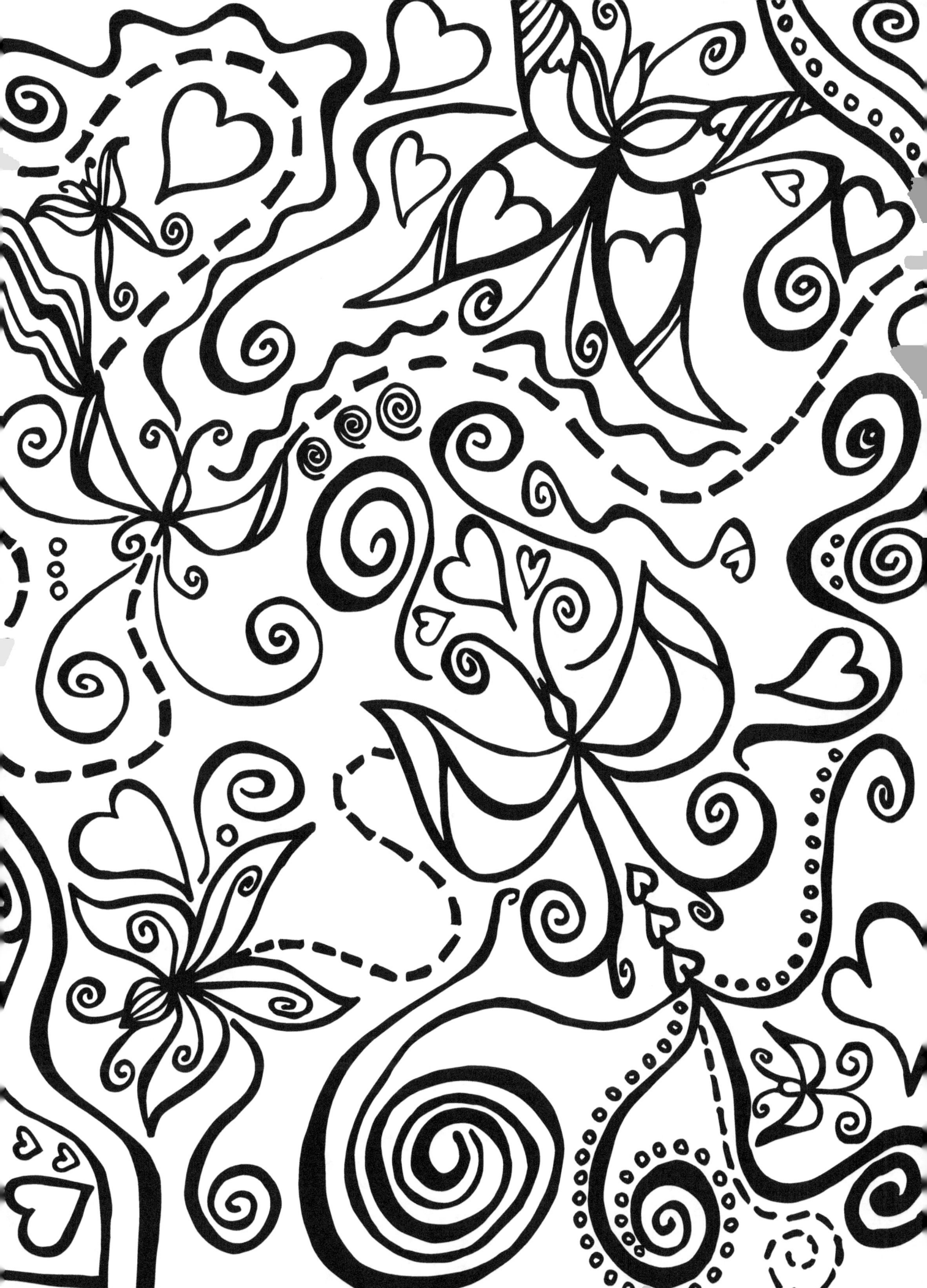

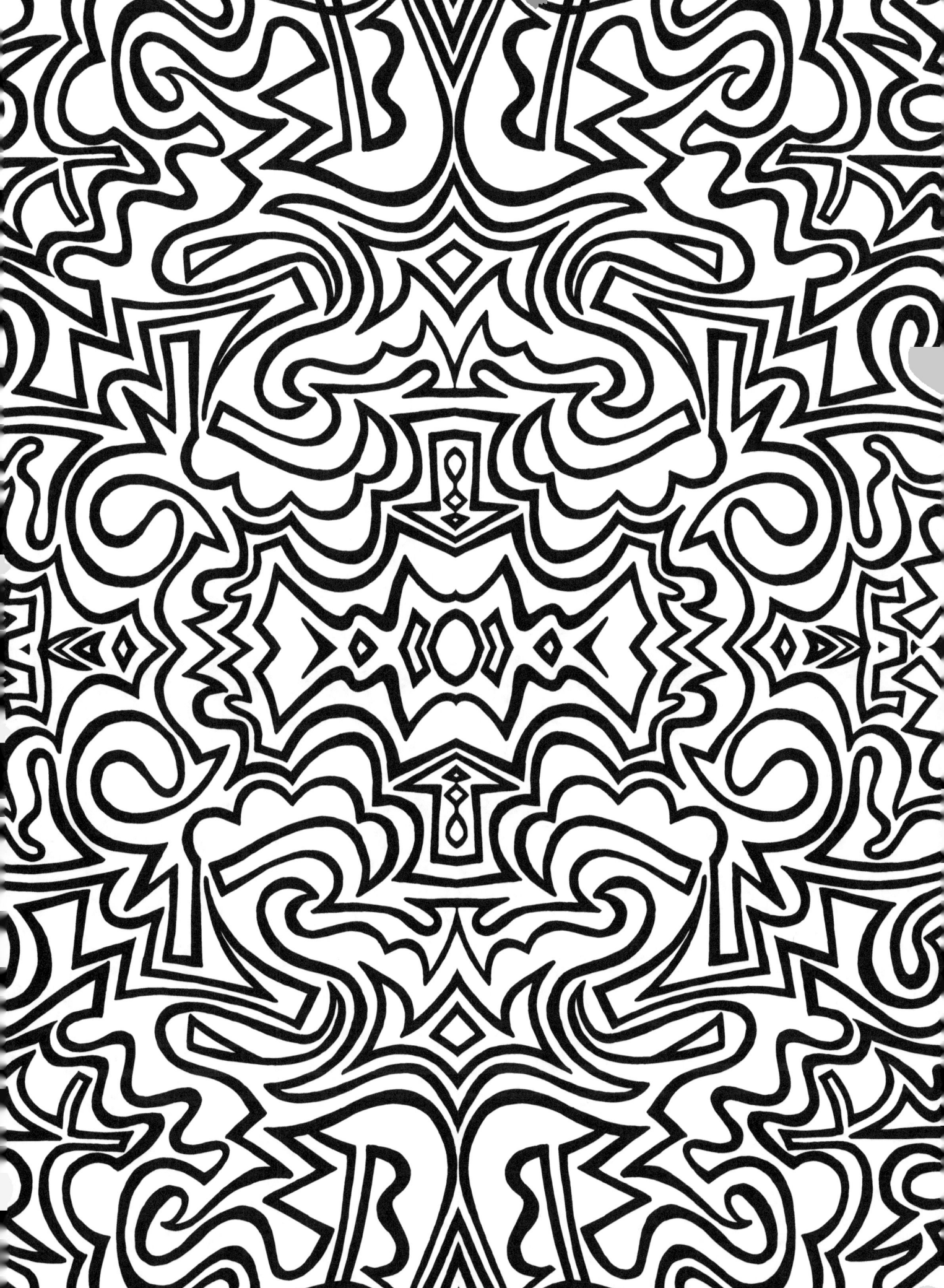

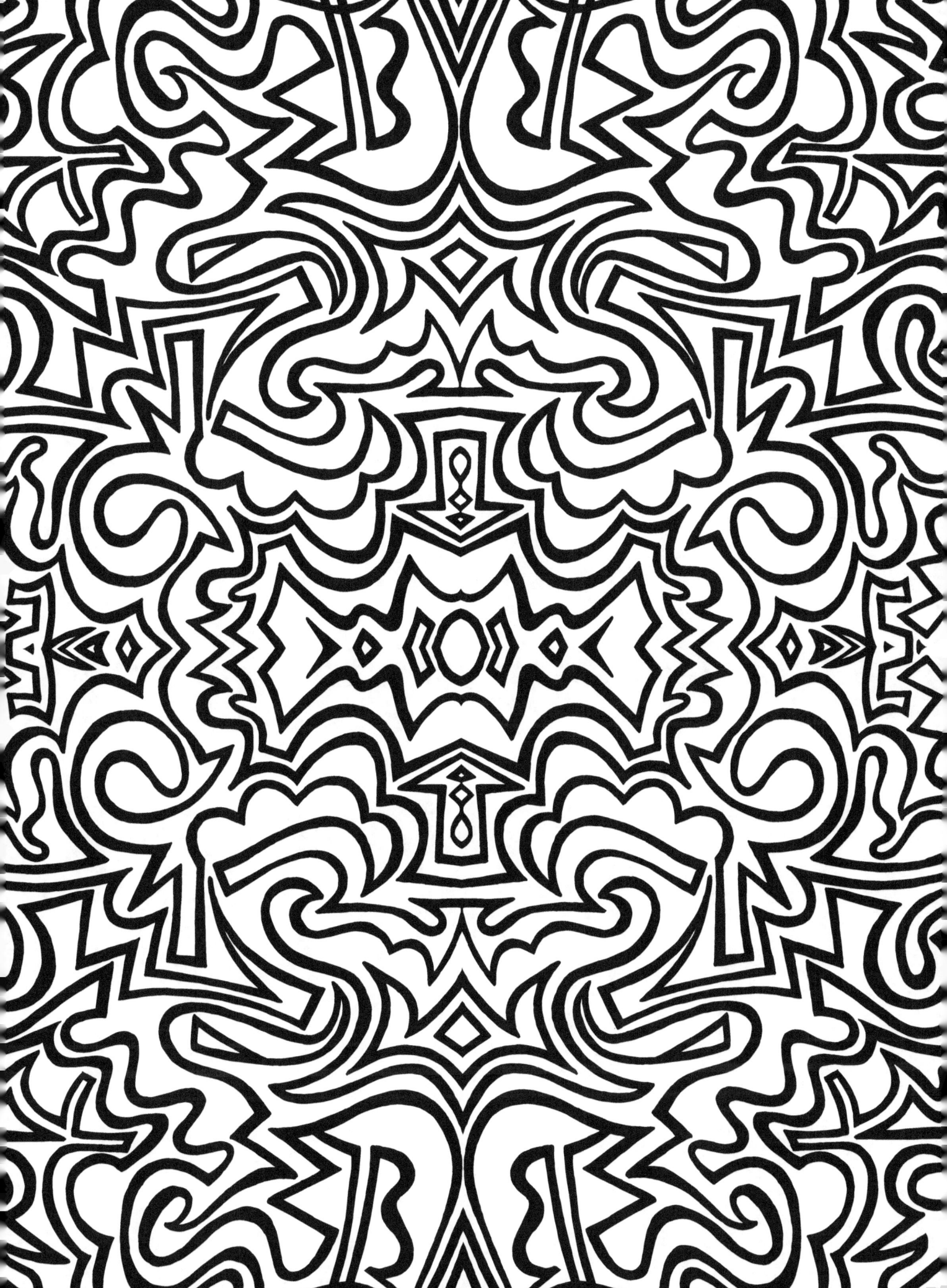

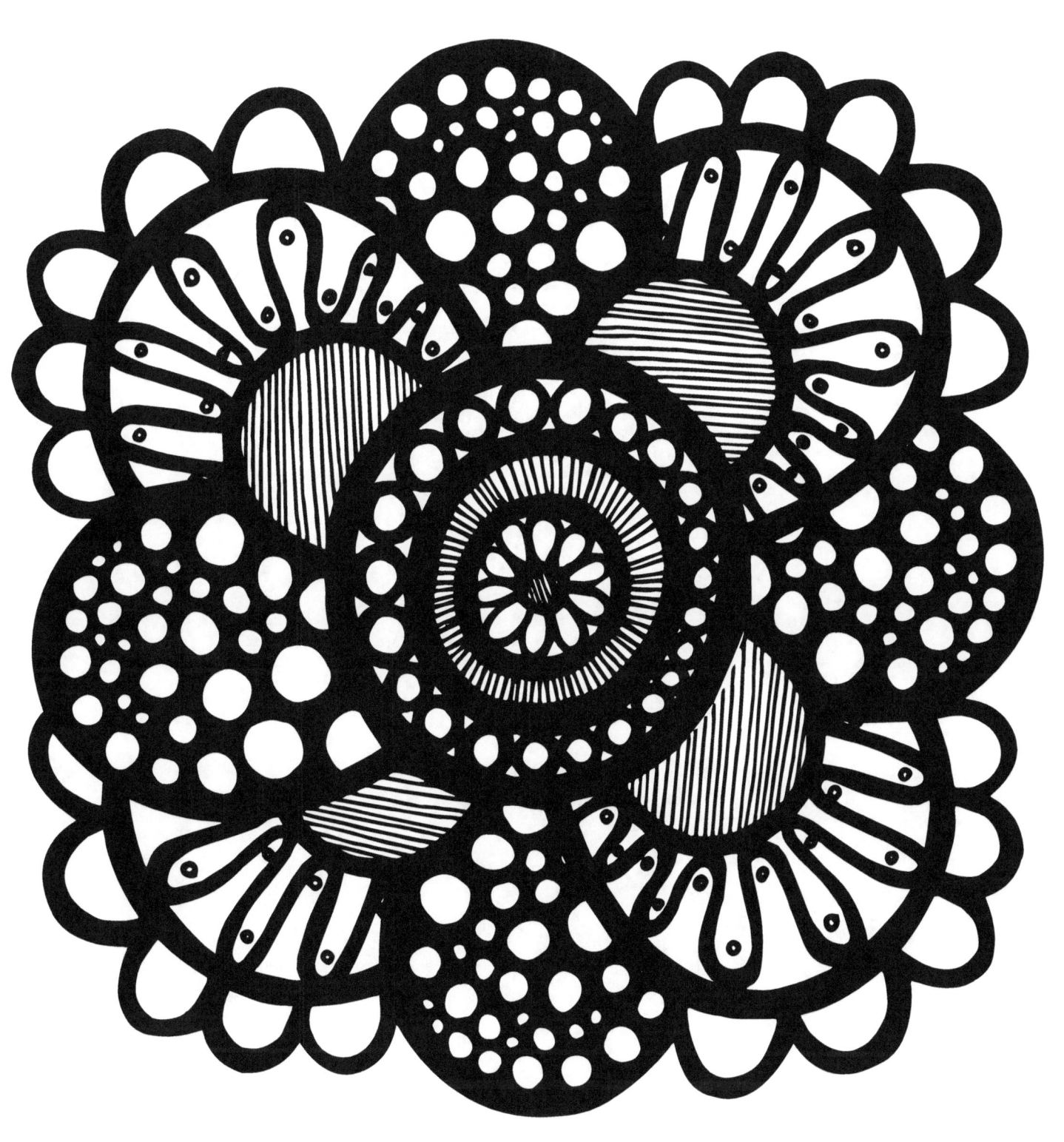

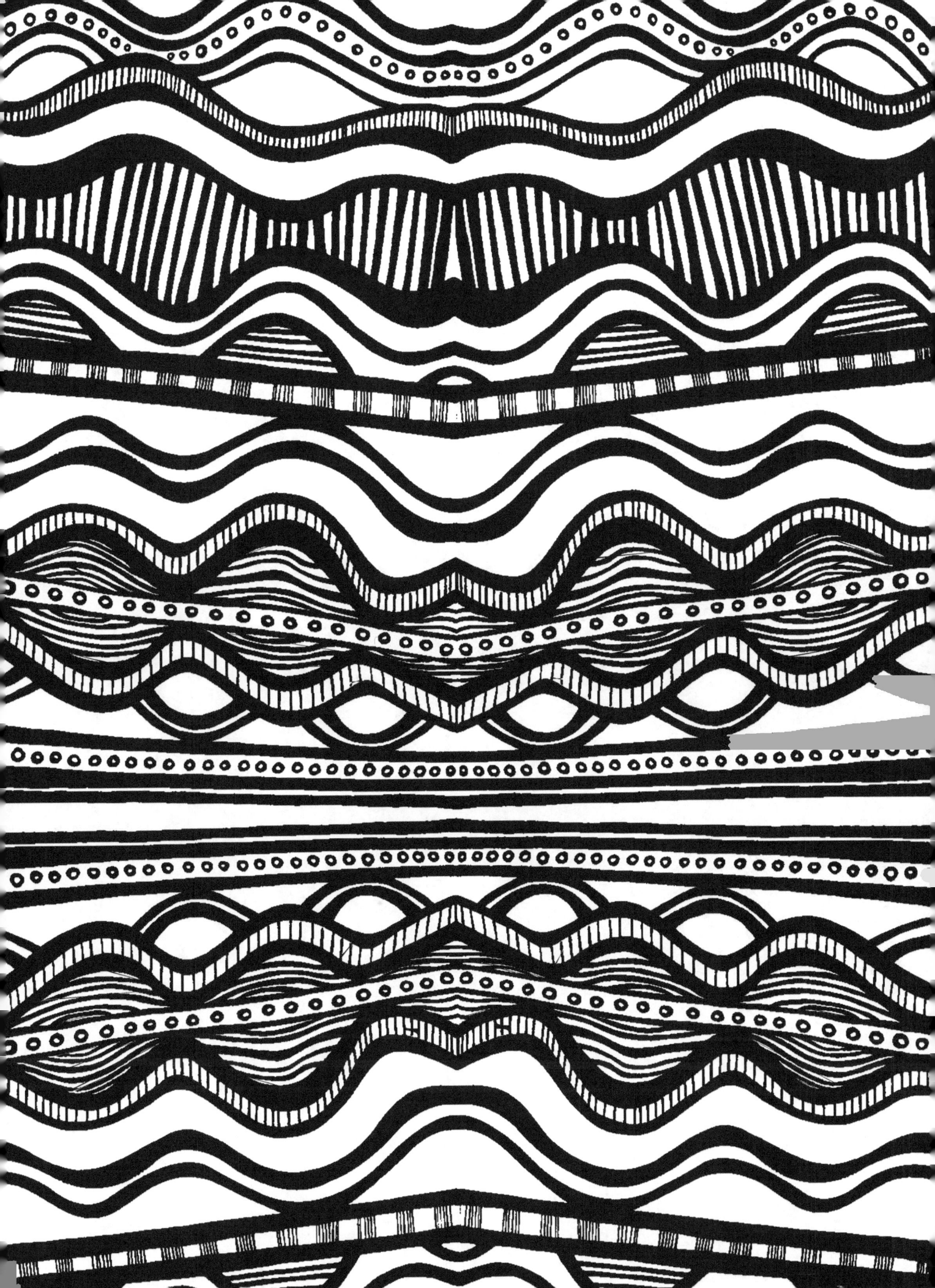

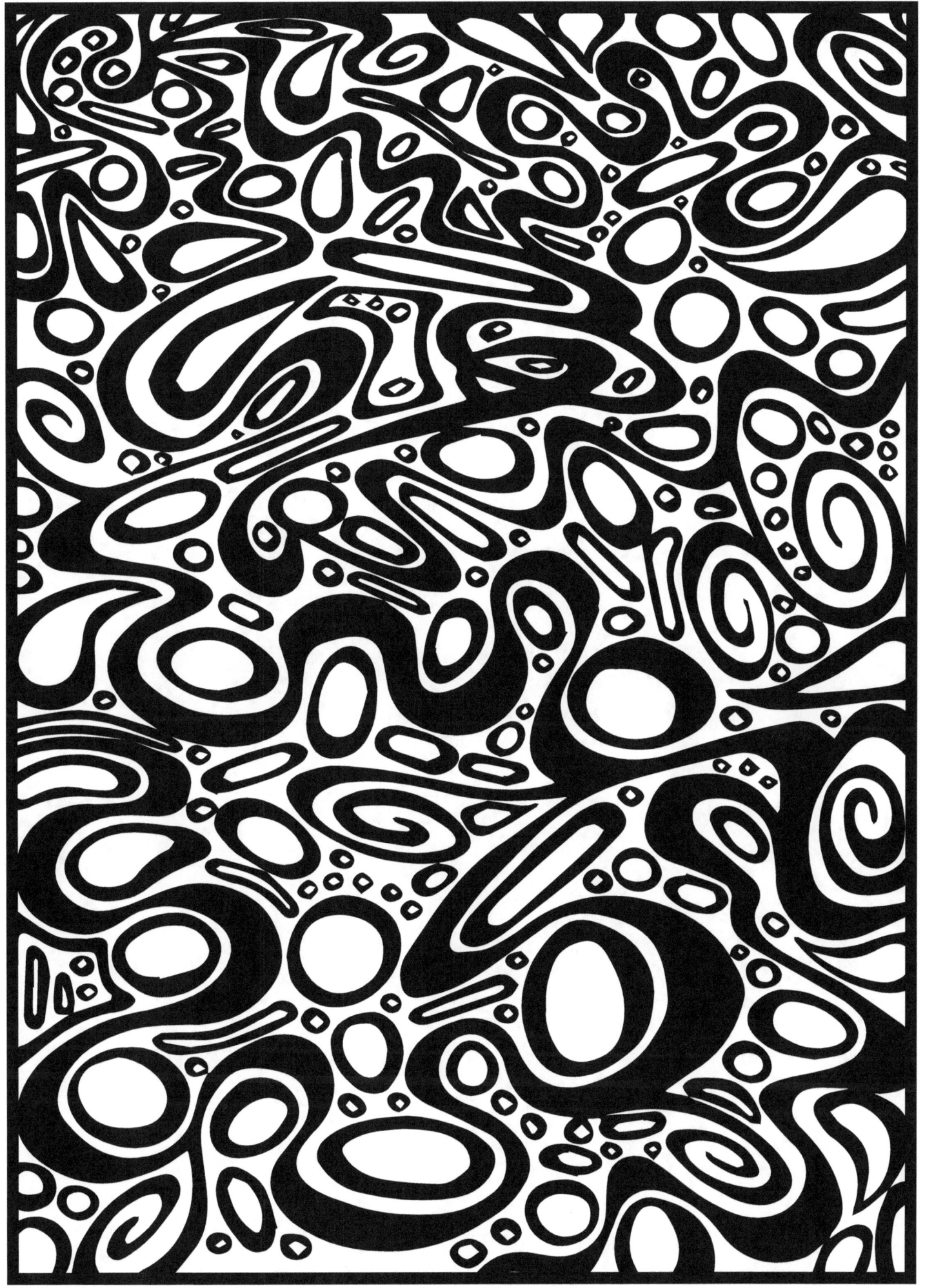

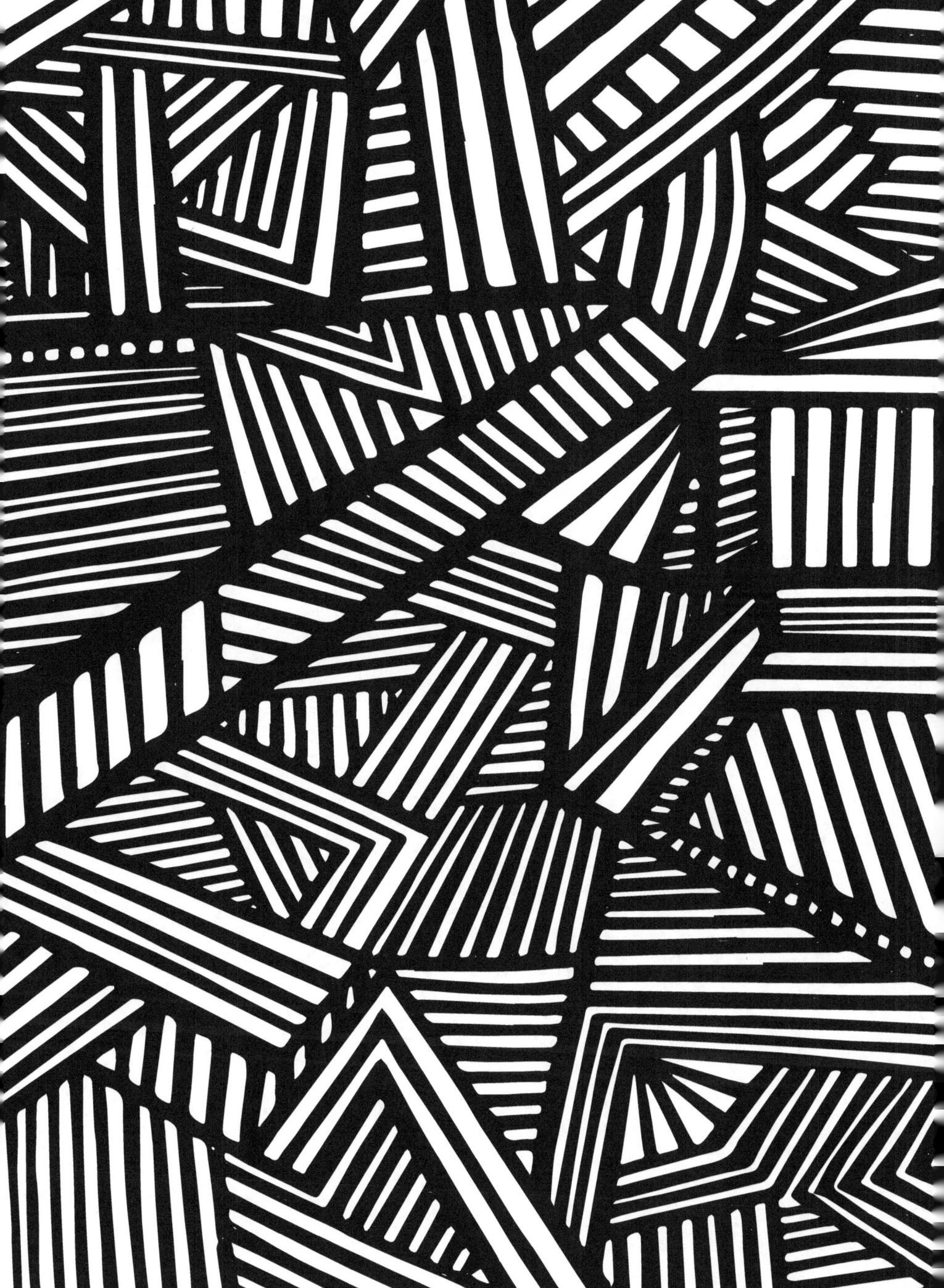

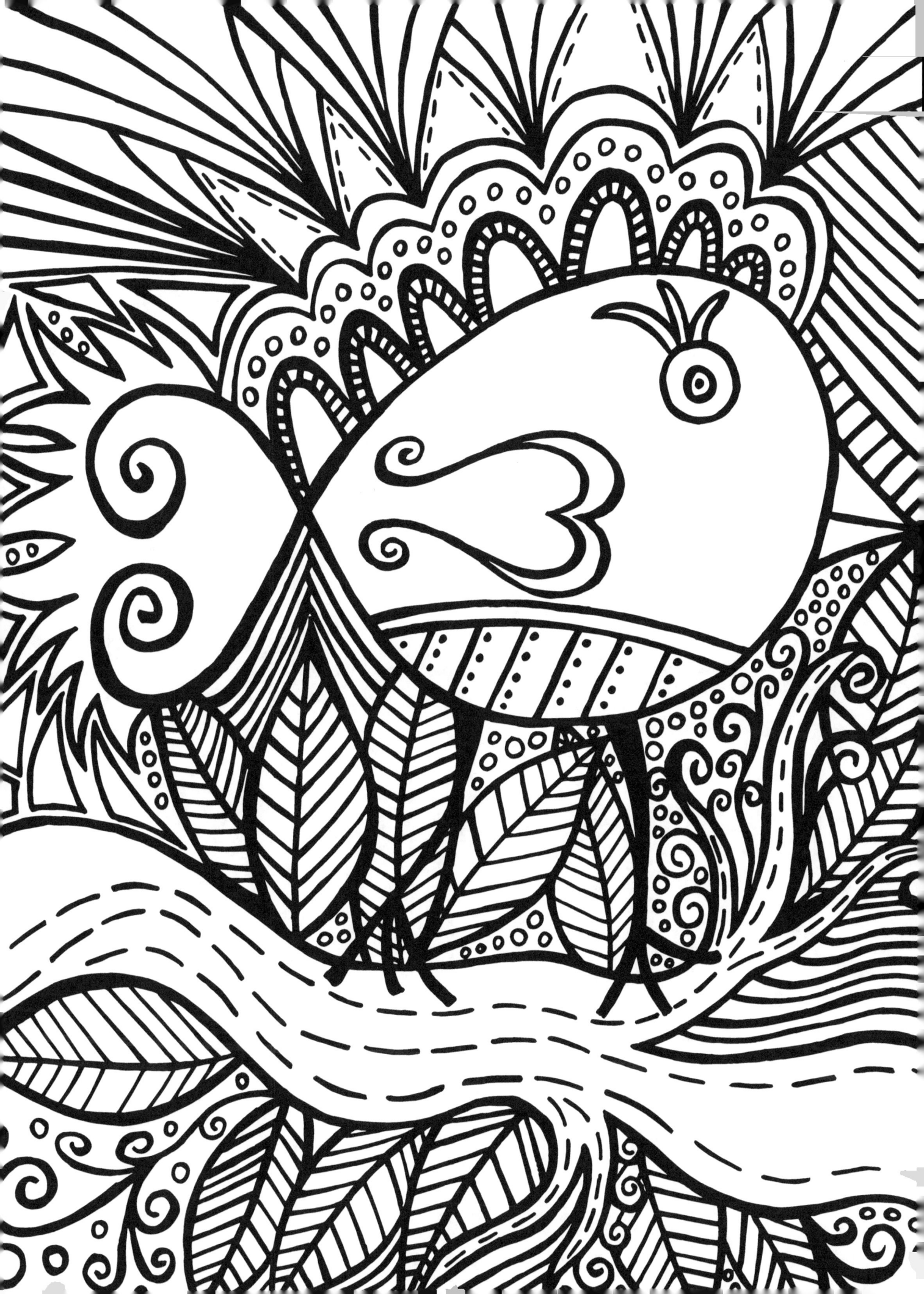

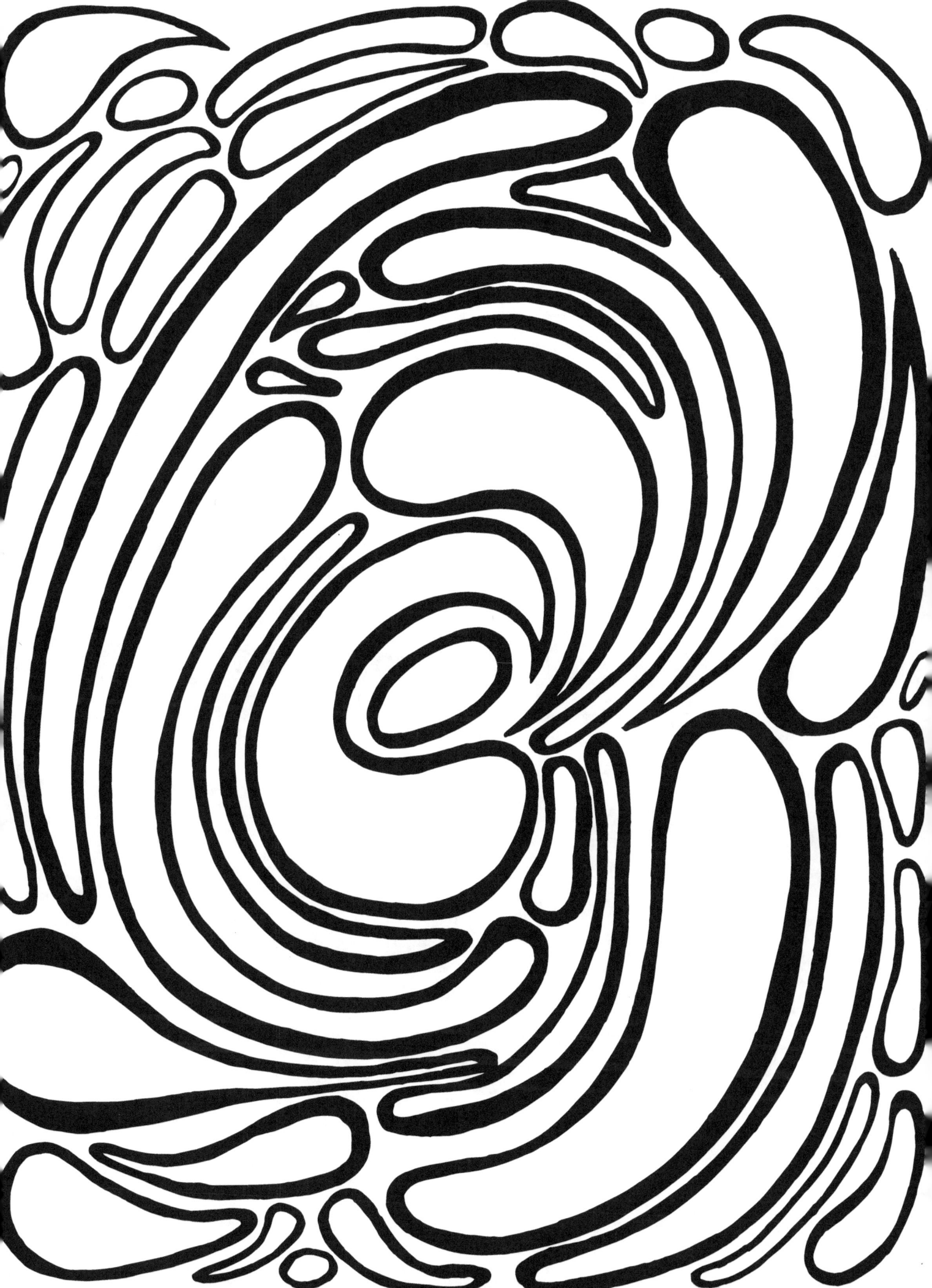

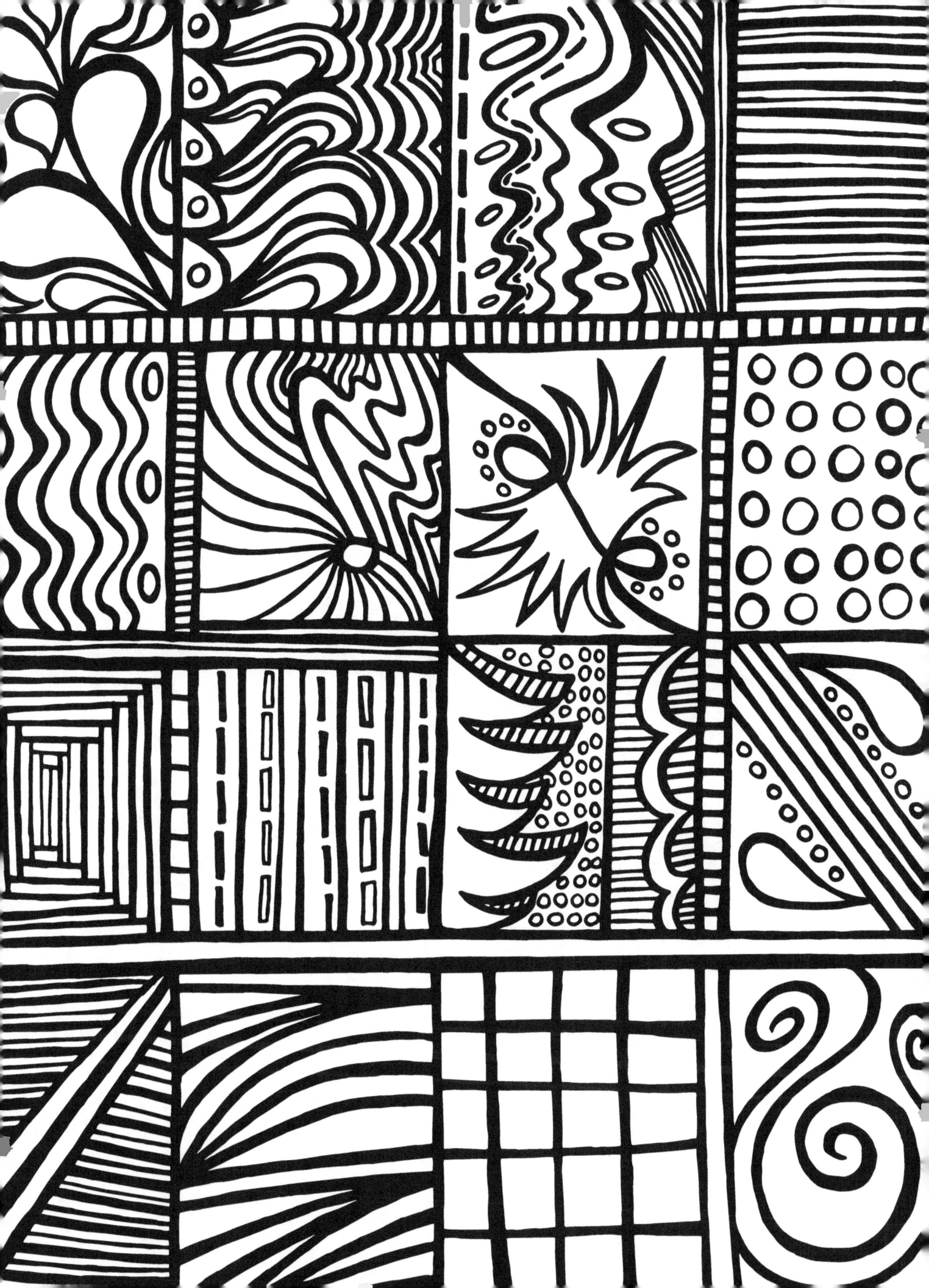

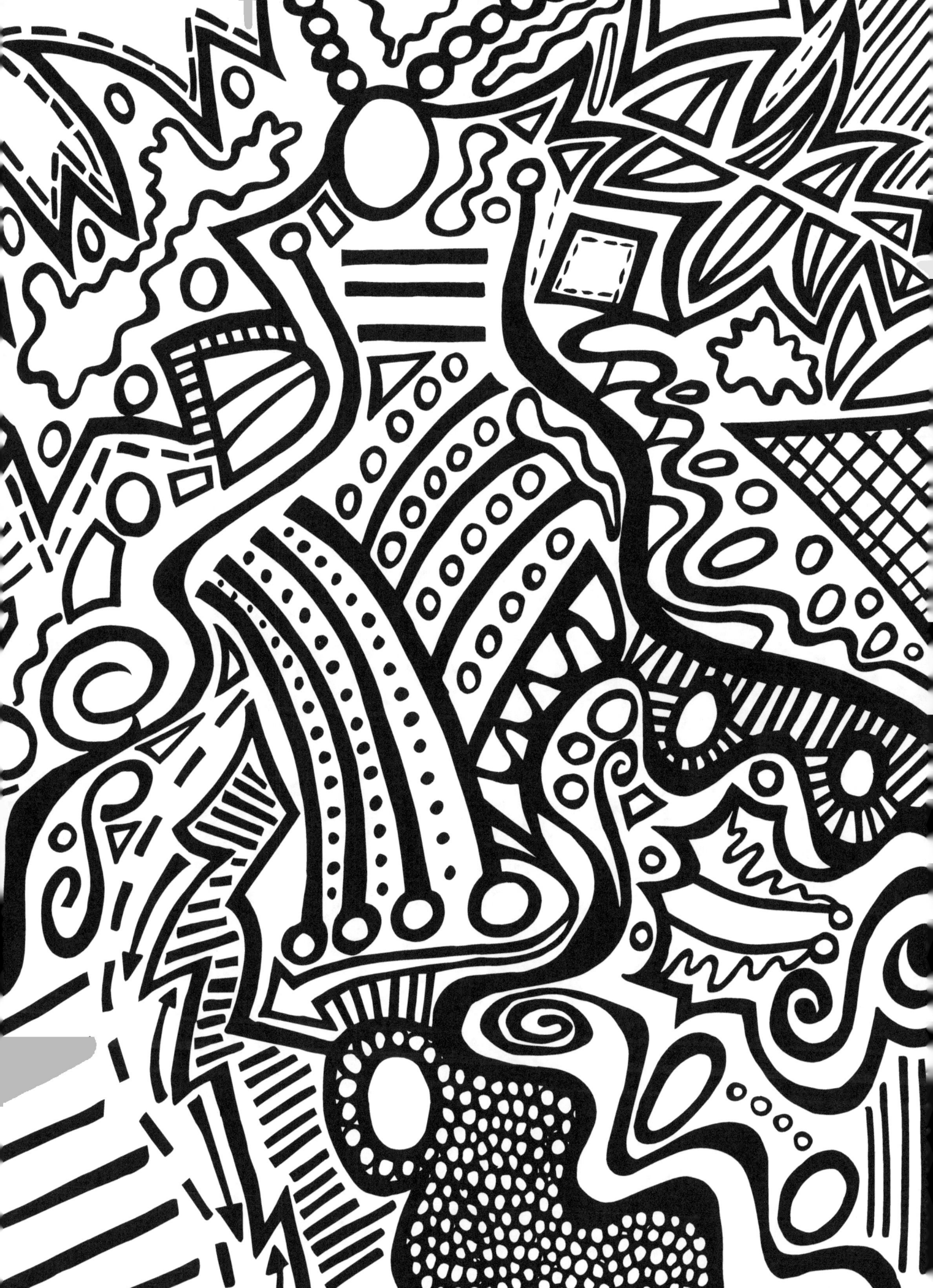

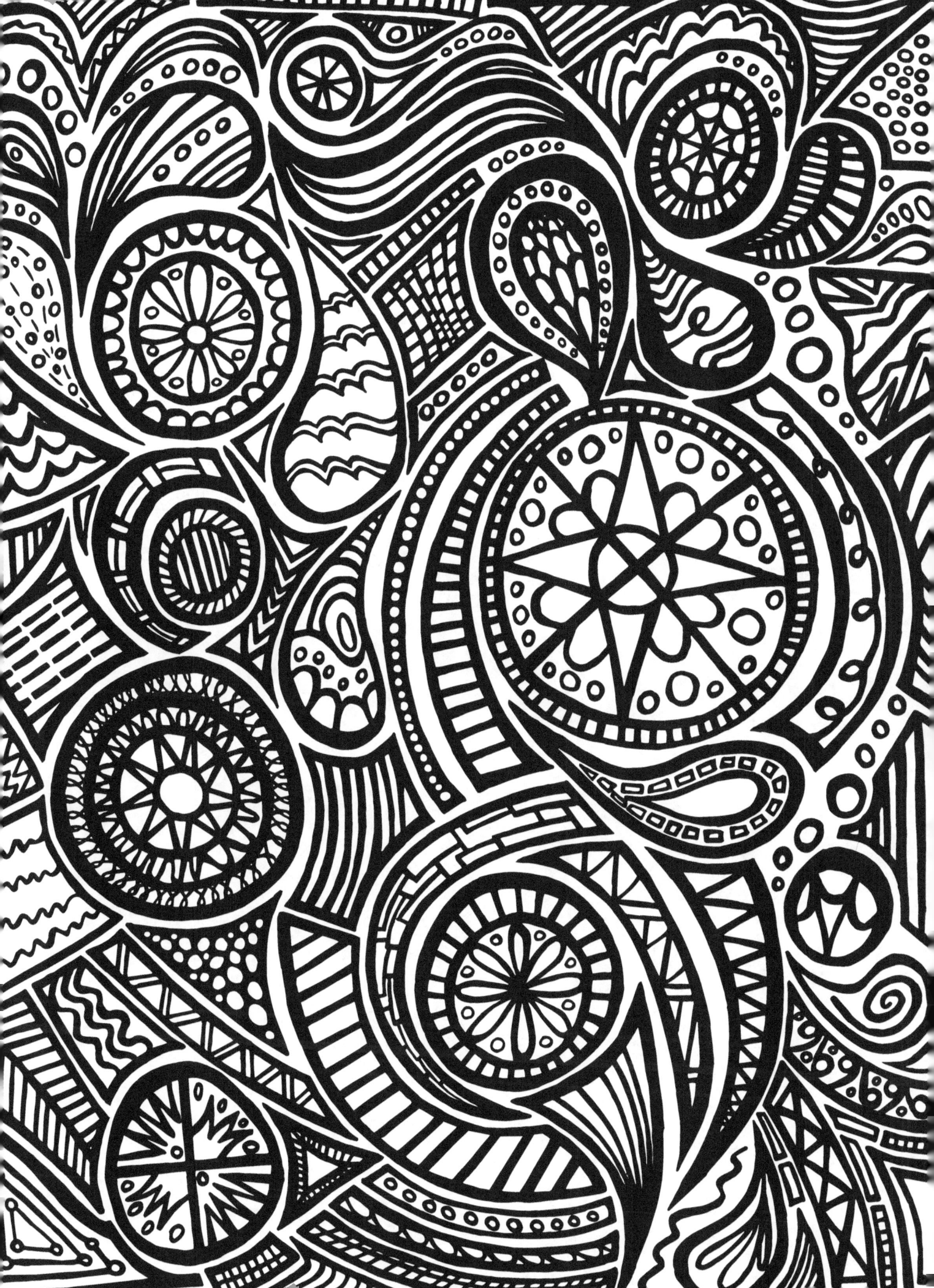

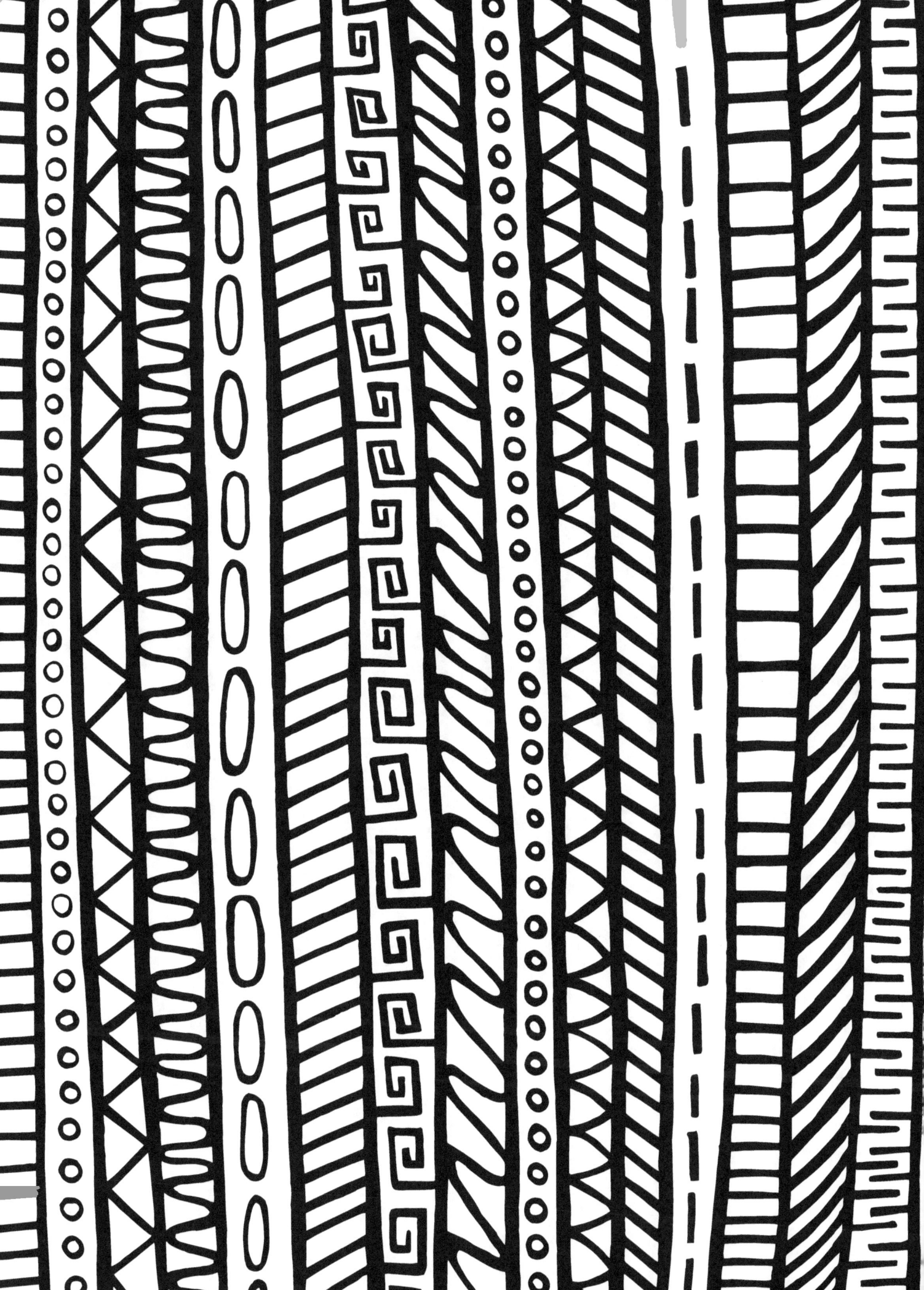

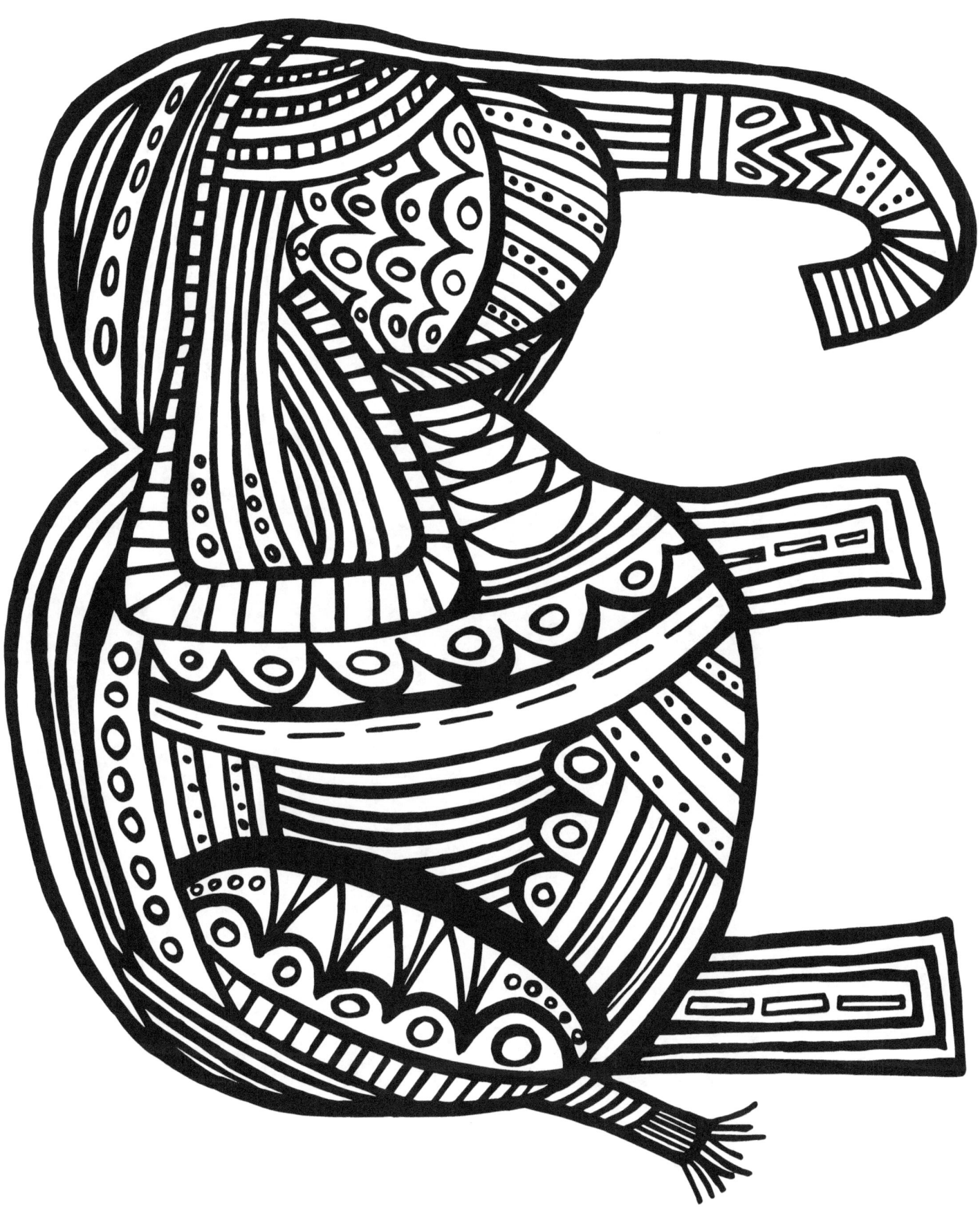

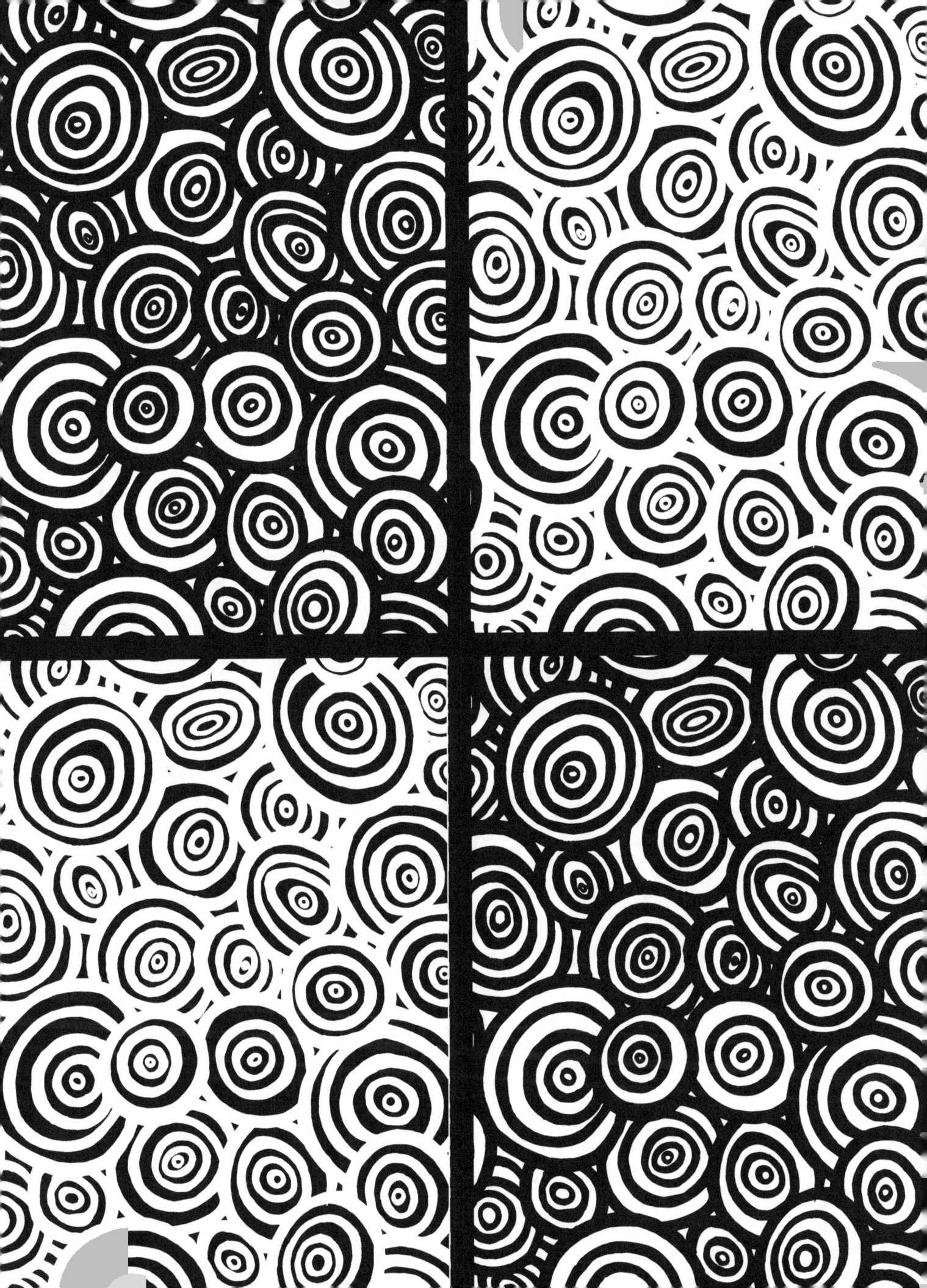

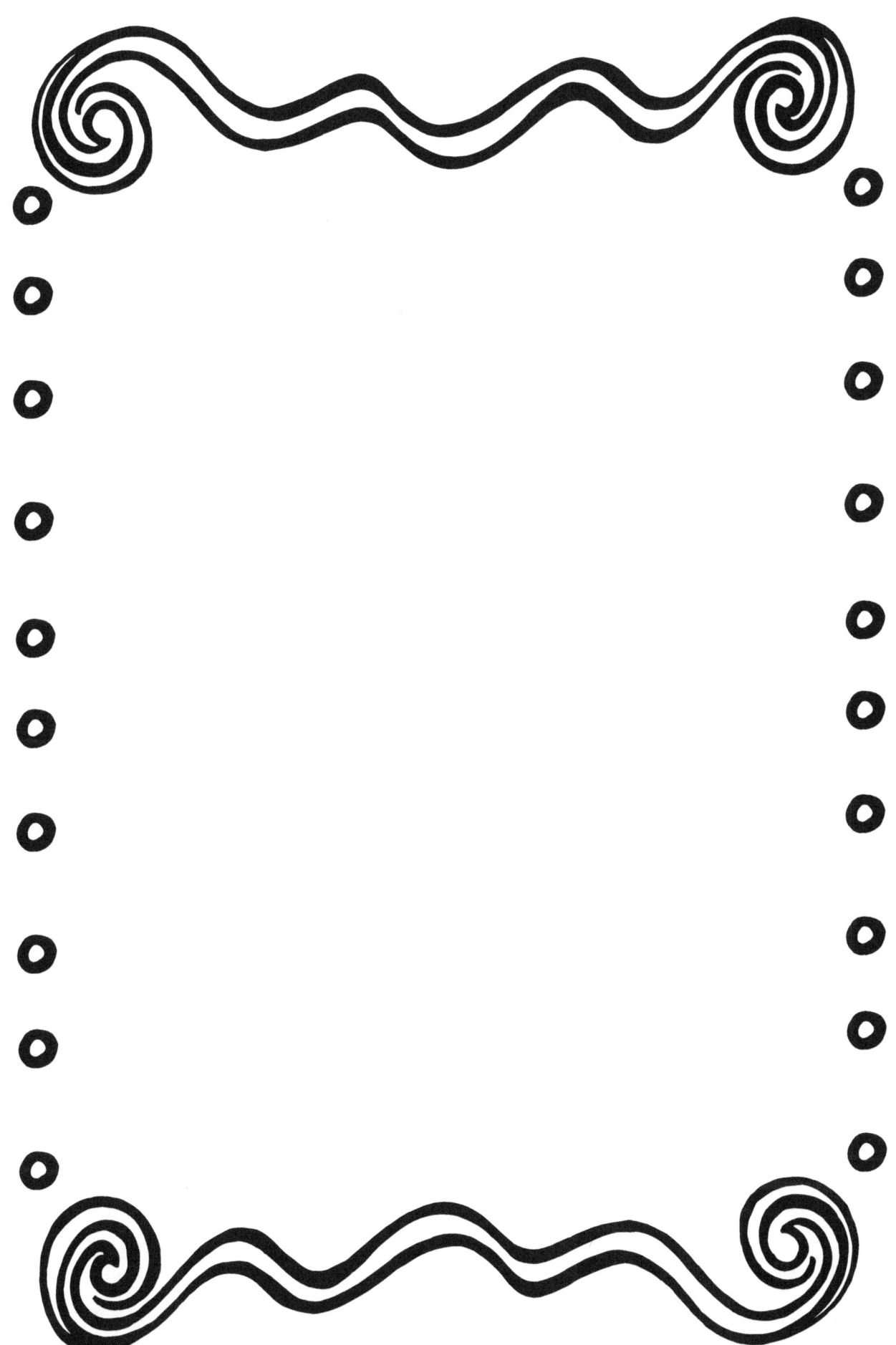

www.ingramcontent.com/pod-product-compliance
Lightning Source LLC
Chambersburg PA
CBHW080644180526
45168CB00008B/3301